TWELVE CITIZENS OF THE WORLD

A Book of Biographies

Doubleday & Company, Inc., Garden City, New York

TWELVE CITIZENS
OF THE WORLD

Book of Biographies by

LEONARD S. KENWORTHY

Illustrated by William Sharp

43435

To Tom, David, and Lee
and their generation—
future citizens of the world

Acknowledgments   The author is deeply indebted to many persons for their help in the preparation of this book. These include scores of friends who have "nominated" various personalities for inclusion in this volume and have discussed the merits of these persons with him. It includes several students who have read the early drafts of several chapters, particularly a group of boys and girls in Mrs. Barbara Allen's class at Midwood High School in Brooklyn.

Help has also come from the editors of *Classmate*, *Forward*, and the *Harvard Educational Review* in whose pages articles on Nansen, Sarmiento, Schweitzer, Toscanini, and Wrede appeared.

Special assistance has come from a notable group of persons who read the chapters on themselves or on a person with whom they were closely associated. Such a list of helpers includes Mrs. Doreen Daughton, secretary to Ralph Bunche; Helene Monastier and Lise Ceresole, a co-worker of Pierre Ceresole and his widow; Dr. Amiya Chakravarty, a long-time friend and associate of Gandhi; J. Henry Carpenter, executive secretary of the Kagawa Movement in the United States; Jon Imbretson of the Norwegian Information Service; Frank McDougall, an Australian friend and colleague of John Boyd Orr; Helen Ferris, friend and collaborator with Eleanor Roosevelt in the writing of their book *Partners: United Nations and Youth*; Margaret Kiser of the Pan-American Union; Emory Ross, executive secretary of the Schweitzer Fellowship in the United States; Dr. Kuo You-shou of the UNESCO secretariat; Walter Toscanini, son of Arturo Toscanini; and Greta Sumpf, author of one of the few printed accounts of Mathilda Wrede. For the chapter on Mathilda Wrede the author has also relied heavily upon the only volume printed in English about her, Lilian Stevenson's *Mathilda Wrede of Finland, Friend of Prisoners*, a book which is now out of print.

To these and other persons the author is deeply grateful. Despite their valuable assistance, the responsibility for statements in this volume rests alone with the writer.

Preface   Near the center of the Capitol in Washington, D.C., there is a place called Statuary Hall. In it each state has placed the statues of two of its leading citizens—two of the men and women of which it is most proud.

These men and women are national heroes in the United States. They serve as symbols of our nation and help to build loyalty to our land and its ideals, just as the flag and national anthem or the Liberty Bell and Independence Hall do.

Gradually we are beginning to create such symbols for the world community. The United Nations flag and the U.N. building in New York are two of these symbols. But there is a need for more.

We need to select a group of world heroes who will also serve as symbols for the world community which we are now trying to create. Such men and women would represent outstanding achievements in helping to build a better world. They would be persons who have made a constructive contribution to world culture.

Perhaps some day the people of the world will decide to start a Hall of World Citizens. In it would be placed the statues of persons who had contributed to the concept of One World. Such persons might be elected by countries or by a panel of citizens from all over the world.

The men and women discussed in this book might well be selected for such a Hall of World Citizens. If so, their statues would be placed in the Modern Wing of such a Hall, for each of them is a contemporary or fairly contemporary figure.

Ten of the persons discussed in this book are men and two of them are women. That is not a good balance, but so far in the history of the world men have made a larger contribution

9

to public life than women. Perhaps as time goes on and women become more prominent in world affairs, the balance will be better.

These twelve citizens of the world come from eleven different countries. Two of them were selected from the United States because this book is being published in that country. Each of the others comes from a different country—from tiny neutral Switzerland, from the huge sub-continent of India, from Alsace which has been a part of France and of Germany in different periods of history, from the recently industrialized island of Japan, from the rugged, mountainous nation of Norway, from the bleak and beautiful land of Scotland, from the vast stretches of Argentina, from the ancient and mammoth nation of China, from that boot-like land of Italy, and from the lakes and forests of Finland. They are also representatives of various areas of the world—Europe, Asia, Latin America, and North America.

By selecting persons from different parts of the world and from different nations, the author has tried to show that world leaders can come from any place. No nation or region has a monopoly on them.

These twelve men and women also represent many different vocations. Three of them have worked in recent years for the United Nations. But before they took on that work one of them had been a scientific farmer and nutritionist, a second was a college professor and diplomat, and the third a housewife and social worker as well as the wife of the President of the United States. One of them was an explorer and scientist. Another was an editor, teacher, and President of the Argentine. Still another was a musician. One of the women was a prison reformer. Two of the persons were largely interested in bringing freedom and justice to the two largest nations of the world

—China and India. Another was a combination of musician, philosopher, doctor, and missionary. Mathematics and international work camps attracted the attention of the eleventh. The twelfth is very difficult to classify for he was interested in cooperatives, in missions, and a host of other things.

You may well ask what they all had in common. Perhaps the answer will come as you read their lives. But here are a few clues. Each of these persons was interested in building a better world. They found different ways of doing it, but each person in this book served humanity as a whole in at least one way.

Then, too, each of them was interested in people. They were artists and scientists in the art and science of human relations.

Each of them was also a hard worker. A few of these twelve might be called geniuses. But not all of them. Some of them were born without particularly brilliant brains. They worked hard and channeled their energies into a few or even one worthwhile cause.

Nor were they always popular people. Some of them were quite unpopular, at least for a part of their lives. And the reason? Usually they were champions of unpopular causes. They were ahead of their times. They were frontier thinkers. Only in a few cases did the public really catch up with the thinking of these men and women during their lifetime.

But they were and are all great men and women. By "great" I mean what Archibald Henderson meant when he wrote his book on *Contemporary Immortals*. In it he defines greatness in this way, "The great man is one who lives for aims other than personal and local ones; who gives himself for posterity; who senses the future and strives for the race's betterment. The great man is one who procures for humanity a larger liberty, a freer release of vital energies, a wider horizon and vaster outlook, a greater and purer happiness, a completer mastery of the forces of nature, and a deeper understanding of mankind." As you read these sketches you may want to come back to that statement and check each person by it.

It is easy to read about such persons and to think that what they accomplished is not for us. Few readers of this book will ever be as well known or as great as the twelve persons in this volume. But it is encouraging to remember sometimes that "The greatest men on earth are men who think as I do—but deeper; and see as I do—but clearer; who work to the goal that I do—but faster; and serve humanity as I do—but better."

It is likely that everyone who reads this book will live out his or her life in a troubled world. It is easy to become discouraged and disillusioned about building a better world. Biographies like these sometimes help us to keep our sense of direction in such unsettled times. As the popular writer Joshua Liebman said recently in his book *Peace of Mind*, "Man loses his sense of direction when the compass of his soul is not magnetized by some great human star within the orbit of his experience." It is the author's hope that these biographies will provide some of the "stars" to which we can look for a sense of direction.

The writer of these brief biographies has taken you into the vestibule. If you want to explore further, you may want to turn to longer accounts of these men and women.

But enough of this introduction. Let us move into the Modern Wing of the Hall of World Citizens and let the author introduce you to some of the men and women there.

Leonard S. Kenworthy

13

TWELVE CITIZENS OF THE WORLD

A Book of Biographies

RALPH J. BUNCHE

Champion of Colonial Peoples

One of the most popular public figures in the United States and in the world today is Ralph J. Bunche. Somehow he has appealed to millions of men and women around the globe and they have made him one of the top-ranking world heroes of our day.

Proof of this fact is found in the more than two hundred invitations he receives each month to speak to all kinds of groups, from schools and clubs to national and international conventions. Further proof is found in the fact that he received thirty-seven honorary degrees from colleges and universities in the four years from 1949 to 1952.

And if this were not enough, he received more than fifty special awards in that same period. They ranged from the Honorary Civic Certificate of Ardmore Junior High School and the Franklin Delano Roosevelt Memorial Award of Midwood High School in Brooklyn to the Spingarn Medal of the National Association for the Advancement of Colored People and the American Brotherhood Award of the National Conference of Christians and Jews. To top all of these he was given the Nobel Peace Prize in 1950 by vote of the Norwegian Parliament.

Surely there is something unusual about a man who has been honored so much. Let's make a visit to his office on the thirty-third floor of the glass skyscraper which houses the United Nations and see if we can discover what is so special about this popular man.

As we enter his large and orderly office, we notice a thin strip of blue cardboard on the door. On it in small white letters are the words "Mr. Bunche." Perhaps this is our first clue. We know that he is really Dr. Bunche, but somehow he prefers the title "Mr." to "Dr."

With a smile on his face he greets us, and then in a quiet voice says, "Why don't we sit down?"

Quickly we have sensed the fact that this is no person to feel timid about meeting, even though he is so well known. So we ask the first question which we had planned ahead of time so as not to be lost with words when we met him.

"Mr. Bunche, we know that you are principal director of the

Department of Trusteeship and Information from Non-Self-Governing Territories in the United Nations. Could you tell us briefly just what that long title means?"

"Yes," he replies, "I'll be glad to try, for not nearly enough people know about this part of the work of the UN. They read about the quarrels in the General Assembly or about the fighting in Korea. But they don't seem to know much about the work of the Specialized Agencies or of the Trusteeship Council. What we are trying to do is to help the two hundred million people who live in dependent territories to live better now and to gain their independence eventually by peaceful means rather than by shedding blood for it."

"That's a simple answer," we say. "But it must be a tough assignment to help them with all their problems of food, cloth-ing, shelter, and the hundred and one other things they need, not to mention their demands for independence."

"Well . . . it is delicate. It is complicated. And in a way it's 'tough,' as you say," Bunche agrees. "But it's important— and it's fun."

He has given us several "leads," but right now we can follow up only one. So we say, "You say it's 'important.' Could you spell that out a bit? Just why do you think it is so important, when you could be doing so many other things in the world?"

He leans back in his chair a minute, thinking, and then the words begin to flow easily and rapidly. "You see, the preponderance of the world's population today lives in Asia and Africa. They are people who have never been accorded their fair share of human dignity. They are people who have had more than their share of colonialism, suppression, and foreign exploitation. They have had far more than their share of hunger, misery, and despair. The Charter of the UN holds out for them the promise of a better life and of ultimate freedom. Our job is to speed that process along as fast as we can."

Just then the buzzer rings and Mr. Bunche excuses himself while he talks to someone in the UN Secretariat about a report from an African tribe of which we had never even heard.

While he talks, we glance at the rows and rows of books that cover one sidewall of a room which must be 18 by 24 feet or something like that. There are books on Africa and Asia, books on the UN and international affairs, books on education and anthropology, books on the Negro, and reports of all kinds on the work of the Trusteeship Council. Our clues are piling up as to the interests of this well-read man.

Apologizing for the interruption, he turns to us again and continues right where he left off. "It seems clear to me that no foundation for peace can be really secure and enduring unless and until the colonial peoples are given a chance to determine their own destinies. There will be no chance for eventual peace in the world until everyone is relatively equal in opportunities."

To ourselves we say, "No wonder Bunche can make speeches, when he can talk off the cuff like that."

We know that he is busy and that we should not take a lot of time, so we shift the conversation abruptly and say, "Mr. Bunche, you've had a fascinating life and you've been around a lot. If you could talk over the radio or television to every young man and woman in the United States, is there any particular advice you would pass on to them from all your experiences?"

He laughs and says, "You know, I've been asked that one

before—several times. A magazine for girls asked me that ques tion a few months ago and this is the gist of what I said: If I had to give today's young people a little bit of advice, I'd say, 'Have dreams—big dreams—but keep the dreams in your head, and always keep your feet solidly on the ground. There are no short cuts, free rides, or sure things in life. And there are no substitutes for hard work, tenacity, courage, and imagination. Be as sure as you can be that you are right and be bold enough to back up your judgment with action—even if that means taking chances.' "

As he is talking we think of Gandhi and when he finishes we say, "That would be good enough to hang over the mirror in our bathroom and memorize, the way Gandhi did with the wise sayings of India." Mr. Bunche tosses his head back and replies, "Oh no, not that good."

By now his secretary is standing at the door and we know that someone else is waiting to talk to him. He gives us a hearty handshake and we say good-by.

Out in the hall we pause and catch our breath. It has been a brief interview, but a memorable one. We have learned a lot about this man even in a few minutes. As we stroll down the corridor and take the elevator down to the dining room, we think about what we have learned.

First of all there was his easy manner and his friendliness. Somehow it always seems that the bigger a person is, the easier and friendlier he is to meet. Bunche had certainly met that test of bigness.

Then there was his quiet humor. He had not told jokes. But he had smiled and laughed. And he had said that his job was difficult but "fun." Imagine having the responsibility for the welfare of more than two hundred million people—and thinking it was "fun!"

Obviously it was a job that he thought important, too. We had given him a chance to mention some of the important jobs he had been offered, like the one in the Department of State or the presidency of the City College of New York, but he had not mentioned them. He had talked about the UN's responsibility for the colonial people. As he talked about these people in underdeveloped countries, he had talked as their champion rather than as their supervisor or guardian or custodian.

That statement about his advice to young men and women was full of "leads," too. He had talked about "no short cuts, free rides, or sure things." We think about that a lot and guess that he was talking out of his own experience. He must have worked hard all his life, especially since he was a Negro and had not had too many breaks because of that fact.

The way the phrases rolled off the tip of his tongue was impressive to remember. He was full of his subject, but also the way in which he spoke was extraordinary. It was quotable. It was crisp. It was well worded.

And then there was that part about having dreams but keeping your feet on the ground. That was the advice of a practical idealist. He wanted freedom for those two hundred million people, but he knew that he would have to proceed cautiously and carefully to secure the breaks for them.

Down in the dining room we talk to some of his colleagues and they have nothing but praise for him. Some talk about the way he works, running circles around them. They tell us he often works late at night, drafting reports and writing speeches, and that he makes those speeches mostly in vacation time or on week ends when he should be resting. Others talk about the way in which he welcomes the inconspicuous people around the UN when they drop into his office to talk about personal, family, or job problems.

All of them agree that he is intelligent, warm and understanding, industrious, decent, sincere—"a good guy."

But this is not enough to explain the popularity of Mr. Bunche. So we burrow around in books and magazines, in newspaper files, and in official documents to find the story of his life. And here it is. In it will be more clues to the development of this extraordinary international civil servant.

Ralph J. Bunche was born on August 7, 1904, in Detroit, Michigan. His grandfather was a slave. His father was a barber and a poor man.

"I can never remember a time when we weren't poor," he has said. "In the summer my sister and I seldom wore shoes. We saved them for school in the fall."

Ralph had to work to help the family. So at the age of seven he was running errands for a grocery store and selling papers on the street corners of Detroit.

But his childhood was happy as well as hard. He and his friends would hike out to Belle Island, go out on roller skates, or get there on their homemade scooters. Sometimes they would cross over to Windsor, Canada, on the ferry. When the circus came to town they would follow the parade, listening to the calliopes. At other times they would squander five cents and go to the nickelodeons—the early-day movies—or they would listen to the German bands.

There was fun at home, too. His mother was very musical

and some of the happiest memories of his childhood are those of song fests with the entire family singing while his mother played. The "Johnson Quartet," composed of his mother's two sisters and two brothers, with Mrs. Bunche as accompanist, practiced in their home, and Ralph thoroughly enjoyed hearing them sing "Toreador," "The Two Grenadiers," or "Sympathy." He confesses, however, that his own favorites were a little less high-brow. They were "Take Me Out to the Ball Game," "After the Ball Is Over," and "Get Out and Get Under."

He liked the music of the organ-grinders, too, and used to follow them whenever they appeared. Years later, he says, he found himself following an organ grinder in Lisbon, Portugal, on one of his many trips abroad—a hangover from those childhood days.

Fortunately there was little race prejudice those days in Detroit. As he expresses it, "Detroit then was almost color-blind."

His mother was not well and so the family moved to Albuquerque, New Mexico, hoping that the climate would improve her health. Within a few months, however, she died. And then, within three months of her death, Ralph's father died.

What a blow for any boy. And what a double blow for Ralph Bunche. These two tragedies were softened a little by the fact that there was a grandmother to take care of him and his sister. And that grandmother was a remarkable woman. To her Ralph Bunche probably owes more than to any other person. But let him describe her as he did to a group of students at Fisk University at a commencement exercise. This is what he said.

"She was a tiny woman, but a personality of indomitable will and invincible moral and spiritual strength. 'Nana' we all called her, and she was the ruler of the family clan. She had come from Texas, married in Indian Territory, and on the premature death of my grandfather was left with five young children.

"Nana had traveled the troubled road. But she had never flinched or complained. Her indoctrination of the youngsters of the 'clan' began at an early age. The philosophy she handed down to us was as simple as it has proved invaluable. Your color, she counseled, has nothing to do with your worth. You are potentially as good as anyone. How good you may prove to be will have no relation to your color, but with what is in your heart and your head. That is something which each individual, by his own effort, can control. The right to be treated as an equal by all other men is man's birthright. Never permit anyone to treat you otherwise. For nothing is as important as maintaining your dignity and self-respect."

Speaking further of Nana, he said, "She told us that there would be many and great obstacles in our paths and that this was the way of life. But only weaklings give up in the face of obstacles. Set a goal for yourself and determine to reach it despite all obstacles. Be honest and frank with yourself and the world at all times. Never compromise what you know to be right. Never pick a fight, but never run from one if your principles are at stake. Never be content with any effort you make until you are certain you have given it the best you have in you. Go out into the world with your head high and keep it high all the time."

What a sage and practical idealist she was. Put the words

"Ralph Bunche" in front of those quotations and you have his philosophy of life,—which he got from a little-known but wonderful woman.

He had a harder time in Los Angeles, where the family moved on the death of his father and mother. There he worked at all kinds of jobs, but they were harder to find because he was a Negro. He delivered papers, worked as a "pig boy" in the composing room of a Los Angeles paper, and was employed as a carpetlayer in the City Dye Works.

There, too, he began to learn about prejudice, intolerance, and bigotry. His first real shock came at a newsboys' outing. It was a wonderful day, for the publishers had bought out all the concessions in the amusement park and the newsboys were having the time of their lives. They rode the roller coaster, bounced around in the midget cars, and stuffed themselves with ice cream and spun sugar. Then came time for a swim. But Ralph and another boy were barred. Negroes weren't allowed to swim in that pool. Bunche has said, "That sort of thing made quite an impression on a lad of fourteen!"

There were other experiences, however, which helped to compensate for these painful lessons in intolerance. One was in school when they decided to have a minstrel show. The interlocutor's spot was of course the coveted role—and this was usually given to a white boy in any minstrel. But this time Ralph was made interlocutor and the white boys were done up in black faces. He has never forgotten that experience, either.

During his high school days Ralph became a real athlete. He was on the football, basketball, and track teams. But his grades did not suffer: he was also an honor student.

Again race prejudice raised its ugly head. When the time came to elect members to the honor society, he was not selected. There was an unwritten law that Negroes could not be honor students! For compensation he was chosen as a commencement speaker—the valedictorian.

Then to cap it all came his farewell from the principal. The valedictory was over and the principal called him into the office. Ralph Bunche has never forgotten his words. "You've made good here at Jefferson High, Ralph, and I'm sorry to see you go. And I want you to know that I have never thought of you as a Negro."

Years later Bunche recalled this incident and in his understanding way commented, "He meant that in a friendly spirit, but it made me realize how deep-rooted and unconscious prejudice can be."

Next came college. Ralph couldn't have afforded to go, but he received scholarship aid for four years at the University of Southern California in Los Angeles and worked hard on the side to supplement this fund. Part of the time he worked as a janitor in the women's gymnasium. He and a friend also bought an old Model T Ford and stuffed it with brooms, mops, and buckets. Then they established a cleaning service for stores, working early in the morning before classes.

Most of the summers he worked on boats which plied their way along the Pacific coast.

There were athletics, too, during those years at the university. In his freshman year he played football, baseball, and basketball, but an injury prevented him from playing football after that. He was, however, able to play basketball and was on the teams which won the California Conference championship for three straight years. Before graduating he received four varsity letters. One more might have won him the coveted scholarship to Oxford as a Rhodes Scholar, for he was nosed out by a fellow student with more athletic awards than his. He graduated *summa cum laude.*

There was time, too, for other extracurricular activities. He worked on the college daily newspaper, was sports editor of the yearbook, and president of a debating society.

At U.C.L.A. he again experienced some race prejudice alongside many instances of genuine democracy. Because of his color, he was barred from one debating society. Several of its members were incensed by this action and resigned, formed another club without these color restrictions, and elected him an officer of it.

During his college days he also was active in the Cosmopolitan Club, which was a forerunner of the International Relations Clubs and United Nations Youth Councils of today. There he met students from other countries and discussed world affairs. According to him, that was probably the start of his lifetime interest in international relations.

Then came postgraduate work at Harvard. Again he was unable to finance this himself, but he was aided by a $1000 gift from a Negro women's club in Los Angeles. And in Cambridge he worked in a bookstore where the proprietor was so nearsighted that he didn't know he was hiring a Negro. When he was told by his friends what he had done, he asked Bunche if it were true. To which Bunche only replied, "What do you think?"

He completed his master's degree at Harvard in 1928 and in 1934 he was awarded the doctor's degree. His written thesis for that degree was "French Administration in Togoland and Dahomey." As background for that writing he took a three-month trip to Africa, including a "never to be forgotten jaunt of one month's duration into the interior of the French mandate of Togoland and the adjacent colony of Dahomey."

The Preface of the thesis states: "This study was motivated by a deep interest in the development of subject peoples and the hopes which the future holds for them." Gradually the direction of his life was being shaped, although he could not have imagined in those days where this interest in Africa would eventually lead him.

Meanwhile in 1929 he had been invited to Howard University in Washington, D.C., as an instructor. From that time until 1950 he was officially on their staff, although he was often away on leaves of absence in other jobs. Howard University had not had a department of political science up until 1929 and Ralph Bunche was the one who organized that department for them. He rose quickly from an instructor's post to a full professorship and chairmanship of the department. His students liked him a great deal, although they knew that he worked them very hard and had great expectations for them.

Most men would have stopped at this point, but Bunche kept on growing and going places. In 1936 and 1937 he took time out from his work at Howard to do further work at Northwestern University, at the London School of Economics, and at the University of Capetown, South Africa, in colonial policy and in anthropology.

During this period he made a special visit to the Kikuyu tribe in Kenya in East Africa, the tribe to which a college friend belonged. The way was prepared for him by his friend, and when he arrived he was greeted by an elaborate ceremony. In his words of thanks for their welcome, he told of his fore-bears who had been taken from Africa to America and made to work as slaves, and of their finally winning independence. He returned now as to his native land. This was well received by the local tribesmen and he was given the name "Karioki" or "He who has returned from the dead." According to Bunche this name was a great aid to him from then on in his travels about Africa, for it meant that he had been adopted by them as one of their own despite his lighter color and his European clothes.

In 1936 the Quakers asked him to become co-director of the Institute of Race Relations at Swarthmore College, outside Philadelphia, and shortly after that he was selected by the Carnegie Corporation to assist the well-known Swedish sociologist Gunnar Myrdal in the most extensive and objective study of the American Negro which has ever been made.

Commenting upon all these "lucky breaks," as some people would call them, Ralph Bunche once wrote, "I have found that if I concentrated on doing a good job on the task in hand, the breaks would often follow. Good luck, I have often found, is an abundant commodity in America, but it is usually the by-product of effort."

The Office of Strategic Services in the United States Government was looking for someone in 1941 to head up their intelligence work in colonial areas and they asked a Harvard professor for names. He suggested Ralph Bunche and Bunche was asked to take the job, but only after Cordell Hull, then Secretary of State and himself a southerner, intervened to support a Negro for this high post in the government. That started Bunche on his public career. Even though he was officially on the staff at Howard for the next few years, he did not actually return. Soon he was made head of the Africa section of the State Department, a job which included preparation for the North African invasion during World War II.

In 1944 he became Associate Chief of the Division of Dependent Area Affairs in the Department of State and in 1945 he was appointed by President Roosevelt as the United States member of the Caribbean Commission.

When the United Nations was formed, he became one of the first members of the Secretariat, which does the day-to-day work for that organization. At first he was Director of the Division of Trusteeship and after a few months was made Director of the Department of Trusteeship and Information from Non-Self-Governing Territories, the post he still holds.

The biggest event in his life came unexpectedly and tragically. When the war broke out between Arabs and Jews over the control of Palestine, the UN intervened. War there could spread and it was one of the major aims of the UN to prevent such conflicts. Count Bernadotte of Sweden was dispatched to the conflict area to see what could be done to mediate the differences. With him as second in command was Ralph Bunche. Bunche had been told that the mission might last three or four weeks. It lasted eleven months.

On September 17, 1948, a car which carried Count Bernadotte was stopped by five men who opposed the efforts to reach an agreement. One of them fired twenty blasts from a Sten gun. One of the UN observers, Colonel Serot, was killed instantly and Count Bernadotte died on the way to a nearby hospital. Bunche arrived at the same spot within a few minutes. He had planned to make this particular trip with Bernadotte, but delays of all kinds since he had left the island of Rhodes had held him up.

Whether it was luck or the intervention of Providence, no one can say. Anyway, Bunche was on the spot and the negotiations had to continue. The Security Council appointed him Acting Mediator. It was a dangerous job but an important one for the peace of the world.

The final negotiations took place on the island of Rhodes, in the Mediterranean—the closest neutral territory. There Bunche worked untiringly, intelligently, patiently. Many a night he and his secretary, Mrs. Doreen Daughton of England, stayed up the entire night working on memoranda after a day of conferences. For weeks they existed on three or four hours' sleep.

Luckily Bunche knew how to relax. When there was a temporary lull in negotiations, he would head for the ping-pong table or the billiard table and forget the negotiations. When he went to bed, he fell asleep immediately. It was a great gift. It was one of the things which kept him going.

This indefatigable energy of his was one of the reasons for the eventual success of the negotiations. He would see the Egyptian delegation, then the Jewish representatives, one after the other, until an agreement was reached on one point. Then he would move on to the next. Often he would hold back a proposal until they had reached an impasse. Then he would produce a formula on which they could agree, playing it as a cardplayer plays an ace.

His knowledge of the ways of the opposing forces was also a trump card. Perhaps luck had put him in this key spot, but years of hard work on international relations and the processes of mediation and negotiation had given him the much needed background. And his various qualities of personality stood him in good stead—patience, persistence, good humor, industry, optimism, tenacity, and tact.

As he recalls the negotiations he says, "Throughout the endless weeks . . . I was bolstered by an unfailing sense of optimism. Somehow I knew we had to succeed." And succeed they did. An agreement was finally reached in 1948 between the Egyptians and Jews and later between the other warring parties. It was an uneasy peace, but it was peace. Bunche knew that the problem of Palestine had not been solved, but he knew that an armistice had been declared and that more peaceful methods could be employed for further agreements.

Speaking to a group of high school students at Westtown School the next year, he told them, "The processes of conciliation and mediation are slow and tedious, but they can pay handsome dividends. In the long run it may well be that they will provide the most firm procedural foundations for a peaceful world."

Further war had been averted. The prestige of the United Nations had been enhanced. The method of mediation had been proved successful in the hands of a skilled mediator.

By this dramatic event Bunche had been catapulted into public prominence. He had become a symbol. He represented the success of the United Nations. He represented the hope of the world for peace. He represented the yearnings of the colonial peoples for a better life. He represented the Negro race at its best and the possibility that it would increasingly be released to make its contributions to a better United States and a better world.

As a man and as a symbol he returned to the United States to have many, many honors heaped upon him. In New York he was greeted with a ticker-tape parade down Broadway. In Los Angeles they honored him with a Ralph J. Bunche Day. Within three months after his return he had received a thousand invitations to speak. Colleges and universities vied with one another to give him honorary degrees. Organizations of all kinds awarded him medals, scrolls, certificates, and plaques.

All these honors would have overwhelmed most men. But Bunche just went on being himself—the modest, warm, genial human being that he is—but also the hard-hitting, courageous, undaunted champion of democracy at home and abroad that he has always been.

He could accept only a few invitations to speak, but he managed all he could, and carefully chose the places where he would appear. One of the most memorable of these was in Springfield, Illinois, on February 12, 1951. He had always admired Abraham Lincoln and had said that the Gettysburg Address is the greatest speech that has ever been given. His own speech in Springfield was also a memorable one. In it he revealed much of his philosophy of life, many of his methods, several of his concerns.

"The world," he said, "is on the threshold of a new age—the atomic age. It can become for mankind an era of unparalleled progress or blackest tragedy. So very much depends upon the ability of governments and peoples to accommodate their thoughts and actions to the radical changes and urgent needs of our times." Such was the state of the world as he saw it and such was the need for adaptability to change as a primary requisite for all persons in this new era.

"In this age," he continued, "the well-being of people must always be the highest consideration. *All* peoples must count equally or quite likely none will count for very much before long." Here was the urgency of the times and the need for a better life for everyone rather than a selected few chosen on the basis of nation, race, religion, or economic or social status. To paraphrase Lincoln, he was insisting that the *world*, under God, should have a new birth of freedom, and that government of the people, by the people, and for the people should not perish from the earth.

Cautiously but courageously he suggested that national sovereignty might have to be curtailed in the years ahead. "The time will come, if it has not arrived, when thoughtful men must ponder whether peace can be made secure without greater sacrifice of national sovereignty; whether national sovereignty is always to be more deeply cherished than collective peace."

Then he predicted on the basis of years of experience in many parts of the world and with representatives of various nations: "The future may well belong to those who first realign their international sights." He was speaking in the Middle West, which has been more isolationist than internationalist, but this warning he had to give.

Like Lincoln he was concerned over the role of the Negro in our national life and he said so in no uncertain terms. "The United States is in the forefront of international affairs today," he began. And then he added, "The eyes of the world are focused upon us as never before in our history. A great part of the world looks to us for a convincing demonstration of the validity and the virility of the democratic way of life as America exalts it. It would be catastrophic if we should fail to give that demonstration. To enjoy our maximum strength we need more *applied* democracy."

Becoming more personal, he said, "I am proud to be an American and I am proud of my origin. I believe in the American way of life and, believing in it, I deplore its imperfections. I wish to see my country strong in every way—strong in the nature and practice of its democratic way of life, strong in its world leadership, strong in both its moral and spiritual values, strong in the hearts and minds of all its people—whatever their race, color, or religion. . . ."

Speaking more directly on the point of race relations, he said that it is our "number one social problem—perhaps our number one problem. It is no mere sectional problem. It is a national, indeed an international, problem."

He expressed gratitude for the improvement of race relations in the South and elsewhere, adding, "But neither can it be doubted that these relations remain in a dangerous state, that they are a heavy liability to the nation, and that they constitute a grave weakness in our national democratic armor."

Bunche pointed out that in the capital city where Lincoln "sits majestically in his massive armchair" at the Lincoln Memorial, he overlooked a city "which stubbornly refuses to admit his moral dictum that the Negro is a man" and a city which subjected Negroes to "segregation, discrimination, and daily humiliation."

Everywhere he went he prodded the consciences of the nation's citizens. In Harlem he asserted that "American society should cease requiring its Negro citizens to run the race of life over a special obstacle course while other citizens compete on the flat. . . ."

But everywhere he went he held out hope for progress, declaring over and over again that "I have enough faith in the potentiality of mankind for good to believe that he can save himself."

And everywhere he went he pled for support for the UN. To the American Association for the United Nations and through them and the press to a nationwide audience, he proclaimed his faith in that organization. "I am confident," he told them, "that the United Nations, with all its imperfections and all its weaknesses, is the sole force in the world today which can issue reliable peace and freedom insurance."

Down in Florida he addressed a state conference of social workers and to them he said, "The UN is not a government. It is not a superstate. It is an international service organization dedicated to the cause of a world at peace. It reflects the universal longing of war-weary people of all races, creeds, and nationalities. . . . Its sanction is in the hearts and minds of the peoples of the world."

The University of Leeds in England asked him to deliver an important lecture there—and he went. He spoke powerfully and eloquently. There, as in other places, he returned to his championship of the colonial peoples of the world, declaring, "What is basically at issue is the right of all people to be free and to live at the least on those minimum material standards which all humans should enjoy." Enlarging on this theme, he pointed out, "Relatively few of the world's peoples enjoy more than meager measure of freedom—and many, none at all. It has been hoarded too long as the more or less exclusive boon of Western, Atlantic-community peoples."

Meanwhile he worked at his day-to-day job at the United Nations, practicing what he preached, doing what he could to bring peace and justice in larger freedom to his two hundred million friends around the world.

As often as possible, when he is not on crusading jaunts across the United States or on duty some place around the world, he slips back to his home in Kew Gardens, Long Island. There he revels in home life with his attractive and able wife Ruth and their son Ralph Jr., and his daughters Joan and Jane when they are back from Vassar and Radcliffe. Together they enjoy music or watch his favorite team, the Dodgers, or just sit and talk. Sometimes they head for New York and a show or the theater, which are other forms of fun and relaxation.

This is the man who is one of the most popular public figures in the United States and in the world today. Some suggestions have been made as to the causes of his popularity, but they have been merely suggestions. No one has ever figured out just what makes him tick—or ever will completely. By now you probably have your own ideas.

PIERRE CERESOLE

Dreamer with a Shovel

Every summer for the last thirty years small groups of men and women and young people have packed their duffle bags and knapsacks and have gone to join an international peace army with encampments in distressed areas all over the world. Some summers they have set off for India to rebuild the villages destroyed or damaged by earthquakes and floods. Other summers they have converged on Finland to help the refugees from the Karelian Isthmus in establishing themselves again in the northern regions of that nation. At other times they have concentrated on rebuilding schools, youth hostels, and homes in Central Europe or on constructing houses in the midst of the wreckage of Hiroshima, Japan.

These small encampments are called international work camps. The campers come from many countries and from many different vocations. They represent different religions and different races. In recent years many of them from the United States have been college men and women who are giving their summer vacations to some practical service to their world neighbors.

For eight hours a day they work with picks and shovels and trowels and wheelbarrows. Then in the evening they often study together. Sometimes they see movies of the country they

are visiting or hear speakers from the local community where they are working. Sometimes the members of the group talk about their home countries and answer the questions which are raised by their fellow campers. Often they discuss world problems. Other times they sing or dance together.

Most of these work-campers have heard a lot of talks about peace. They have read a good many books on peace. They have attended conferences and classes where peace was discussed. But the work camp is a chance to *do* something about peace. Here is a practical approach to international understanding— a chance to be pick and shovel ambassadors to some foreign country. Here is an opportunity to contribute a little towards bettering international relations and to learn a lot in the process.

No wonder that these camps have become so popular that there are now several thousand young people taking part in them each summer, and several thousand more high school and college young people taking part in week-end work camps during the school year in their home countries.

The success of this world movement is largely due to the efforts of one man, Pierre Ceresole, the founder of this international peace army. He is little known to most people in the world, but he was certainly one of the most practical idealists of our generation and a real citizen of the world. His life was an unusual one and one well worth telling.

Pierre Ceresole was born on August 17, 1879, in the suburbs of the beautiful city of Lausanne, Switzerland. His family was a prominent one in that small but significant country. For several generations it had produced doctors, ministers, lawyers, and statesmen. His father was for several years a federal judge and at one time President of Switzerland.

His boyhood was a very normal one with school and games, hiking and boating, church and family affairs with his brothers and three sisters, and all the other activities of small boys in any land. At the age of nine he lost his mother and from then on he was raised by his oldest sister and relatives and friends of the family.

Pierre was like a great many other boys in his dislike of school. He made excellent grades and was popular with his classmates because of his ingenuity and humor, but didn't like to be confined in school so much of the time, especially in schools where the discipline was very strict and the subjects pretty much unrelated to his everyday life.

From the stories of his family and friends he was a boy who enjoyed life and had lots of fun. But he had a serious side, too. At the age of seventeen he had a particularly impressive experience when walking through the woods. Later on he referred to it as "a solemn consecration to Truth." Writing about it he said, "The thought came to me of some kind of ministry where we would have to recognize first all our own errors, our own shortcomings, in order to be able to be true. I was seized by the discovery that to do something constructive in the world one had to be infinitely more sincere, more true, more direct, more alive than the church people, for instance. . . . I always remembered that particular day in the woods as a highly important day in my life, as if I had met somebody.

The years sped along and he had soon completed his training in mathematics and philosophy at the famous Federal Polytechnic in Zurich in the German-speaking part of

Switzerland. Then he went on to Göttingen and Munich in Germany to study further and to obtain his Ph.D. degree. Germany at that time was the leading country in the world in science and Ceresole was able to study with several famous teachers, including Roentgen, the discoverer of the Roentgen or X ray.

His education completed, he was invited to become an assistant professor of physics at his alma mater in Zurich. He was considered a brilliant mathematician and a promising scholar. Everyone predicted an outstanding career for him.

He longed to see something of the world and especially the United States. So he set out for a four-week vacation in the States during the summer of 1909. What was to have been a short holiday eventually turned out to be a five-year trip around the world, terminated by the opening of World War I.

The visit to the United States was his first big adventure in broadening horizons. He left New York City without money, determined to earn his way as he went. He was a college professor and had worked more with his head than his hands. Now he wanted to earn his way as a day laborer.

The jobs he found were extremely varied. For a while he worked on a poultry farm counting eggs. In other places he worked in the wheat fields and on other types of farms. At another time he worked at a California oil well, where he became a supervisor.

In this way he came into contact with all kinds of people and his education in human relations was a full one.

Once he reached California he began to think about crossing the Pacific. Travel was exciting, exhilarating, and educational. Why should he return to Switzerland?

So he started out for Japan, stopping for some months in Hawaii. There he earned his way by teaching French literature in the University of Hawaii and giving private lessons as a tutor.

There, too, he came across the writings of Emerson, purely by chance. Browsing in the library of the university, he happened to pick up a volume of the *Essays* and was captivated by them. Writing about this experience some years later, he said, "To become acquainted with such a person is an extraordinary experience. He is a vital, living person. He was the first person I had ever met who gave me the impression that he really believed in God." He recalled this experience of discovering Emerson as one which was profound and revolutionary.

What impressed him most about Emerson was his fresh approach to life. Emerson was a rebel against the society of his day, and that appealed to Ceresole. Emerson was interested in experience and action, in abolishing war as the next great task after the abolition of slavery, and in experimenting with new ways of living the good life. All this appealed to the young idealist from Switzerland.

Ceresole read and reread this great writer's thoughts and mulled over their meaning. Emerson spoke to him as no one else had done. Later Ceresole was to experiment with a new method of promoting world peace. But that idea had not been born when he left Hawaii for Japan.

In Japan he worked for two years as an engineer in the office of a Swiss firm, Sulzer. Then came word of the outbreak of World War I, and he made his way back to Switzerland via Ceylon and the Suez Canal.

When he returned, his friends found that he had changed

considerably. He had a new perspective on the world. His outlook was global. He was now a citizen of the world. Most of them were shocked by the change. They were appalled by his nonconformity.

They were all the more shocked when he began to act upon his new ideas. The first such action came in 1916 when he inherited a large sum of money upon the death of his father. Pierre says that this money "burned his fingers." He felt that it was wrong to have money which was not earned. He therefore informed the government that he would not accept his inheritance. Instead, he wanted the money retained by the Swiss Government.

The government was surprised and a bit baffled by his request. They even wondered if the young man was insane. So, just to be sure, they conducted a private investigation. When they discovered that he was perfectly sane and completely sincere, they accepted his gift.

Later on he was to think a great deal about the principle of inherited wealth and to become even more certain that it was wrong. "To live on one's invested income is as debasing," he said, "as to own slaves. In fact, it is the same thing." At another time he declared, "The greatest luxury a Christian could afford would be to get rid of his money if this money were a barrier between himself and other men." Like Gandhi and a few others, he believed that he could work better with all kinds of people if there were no barriers of wealth between him and them.

His ideas on war and military training had also changed during these years abroad. For many years the Swiss had accepted military service as a duty of every male citizen. Many considered it a school of citizenship in which men from different parts of Switzerland became acquainted with each other and in which people of all classes mixed freely. Conscription was and is an accepted fact among them.

But a Swiss teacher named John Baudraz felt otherwise. He believed that it was wrong for a Christian to take part in war and he refused to do military service.

Pierre agreed with him and said so publicly. This was a great shock to his family and to his friends. His father had been an officer in the Swiss Army and one of his brothers was an officer. In 1913 Pierre had even sent a small sum of money from Japan to be used for the aviation fund of Switzerland. His support now of a man who refused to serve in the Swiss Army disturbed his family and friends and they pled with Pierre to retract his support of this "disloyal Swiss," as they called Baudraz.

But Pierre was clear on this point. Because of a slight physical disability he was not required to undergo military training, but he did refuse to pay the military tax. The result was his first prison sentence in 1916, the first of at least fifteen such imprisonments during his lifetime, most of them for refusal to pay this same military tax.

An even more serious consequence of this decision was his sacrifice of further appointments in any Swiss school, for no one who had been imprisoned was allowed to teach in a public institution. This, however, did not deter Pierre Ceresole from doing what he thought was right.

As the war wore on, he became increasingly disturbed by the loss of life and property and liberty in the countries involved in it. More than that, he became disturbed by the way in which Christians on both sides of the war approved of it and fought each other while they prayed to God for success.

Finally he could contain himself no longer. At the end of the regular church service in Zurich on November 18, 1917, he rose and protested that Christians should not support such mass murder. In a firm voice and with complete conviction he declared his refusal to support militarism anywhere and called upon the pastors of all the various Christian churches to join with him.

The congregation was shocked by such words, but the pastor permitted him to complete his statement. Later in life in a somewhat similar situation he was not to receive such kindly treatment.

Up to this point Pierre Ceresole had been chiefly a protester. His approach had been largely negative. In 1919 he attended a conference of the International Fellowship of Reconciliation at Bilthoven, in the Netherlands. There he met men and women from several church groups who felt as he did.

It was at this conference that a German expressed his desire to go to France to help repair with his own hands some of the devastation created by German soldiers including his own brother.

Pierre Ceresole saw in this gesture the possibility of a new kind of service, a civilian service for peace, "the moral equivalent of war" about which William James had written.

This was a novel idea. Here was a constructive alternative to war for those who could not participate in military service. It was to this idea of an international voluntary service for peace that he was to commit himself for the rest of his life. He was no longer to be merely *against* war, he was to be *for* peace through constructive service.

The Quakers had carried on such work during World War I but they had limited their work largely to wartime and their personnel to British and Americans. The idea of "Service Civil International," as it was to be called hereafter in French, was to carry on such activities in peacetime with people from various countries, races, religions, and vocational backgrounds.

The first international work camp was established at Esnes, near Verdun, France, in 1920. For five months a small group of men from Austria, Germany, Hungary, the Netherlands, Switzerland, and the United States filled up the holes made by mines and shells, repaired a road, cleared the foundations of the village hall, and built barns and houses. Pierre Ceresole was in charge of the group and with him for part of the time was his brother, who was a colonel in the Swiss Army. Most of the group, however, were pacifists or conscientious objectors to war. The money for the project was largely furnished by a Dutch woman, with some help from the French Government.

In the next few years there were many opportunities for service. One was in France, another in Liechtenstein, and several in Switzerland. Some of the work was the repairing of damage done by avalanches; some of it repairs of damage from floods.

In each instance the work was done on a volunteer basis except for the minimum requirements of simple but healthy food and the simplest kind of shelter. Often the local people helped with the work for provided quarters for the workers. In most of the camps there were women volunteers as well as

49

men. In each instance the campers were from several nations.

Ceresole had not forgotten during these years that it was still impossible for a person to substitute some kind of peace service for the military service required in Switzerland. He felt that everyone ought to be willing to give some form of service to his country, but that provision should be made for those who could not conscientiously perform military service. In 1921 he led a movement to provide an alternative service, and forty thousand signatures were obtained and submitted to the government. But the government ignored the petition for months Finally, in 1924, it was officially rejected. Repeated efforts have been made since that time to establish an alternative service, but each of them has failed.

In 1928 there was a terrific flood in Liechtenstein, a small country between Austria and Switzerland. To that tiny principality went 710 volunteers from 22 countries and from 50 professions, trades, and occupations. For six months they worked to reclaim 100 acres of land and succeeded so well that the yield was trebled by their efforts.

Two years later more than 250 persons traveled from 16 countries to the village of Lagarde in France to repair the homes which had been damaged by the spring floods. When the work was completed, a small sum of money was left in the treasury of the work camp group. They turned this over to the village and years later some of it was sent to Wales for use in a work camp there among unemployed coal miners.

Then came the world-wide depression and the idea of the work camp really took hold in England, with some modifications. In order to involve more persons and accomplish more work, many of the campers took part during their vacation periods and there was consequently more turnover in the personnel of the camps. This meant that camps sometimes lasted for only a week or two weeks or that different groups of persons were in the same camp over a period of several weeks.

But the camps remained coeducational, volunteer, with emphasis on simple forms of labor so that untrained persons could take part. Most of the campers were of college age, but there were some older people who helped. Particular attention was given to work in the coal-mining areas where the work campers assisted in garden projects to increase the food supply for unemployed families. Other camps worked with refugees from Central Europe or assisted in the building and repair of youth hostels.

During the 1930s the work of the Service Civil International was extended to India. In 1934 an earthquake of alarming proportions took place in Bihar in northern India and many villages were destroyed or greatly damaged. In addition, there were terrific floods and many of the villages had to be removed to higher land, or dikes had to be built to protect them.

This work in India was another adventure in international friendship. As president of the Service Civil International, Ceresole made four trips to that country in 1934, 1935, 1936, and 1937. With him on the first trip went another Swiss citizen and two Englishmen. On subsequent trips he had as companions citizens from several European countries and from the United States.

Especially dear to his heart was the building of Shantipur, the Village of Peace. At this site homes were rebuilt and simple flood control measures were inaugurated by the small group of foreign volunteers and by the Indians. In addition, progress was made in building a community which could serve as a model for the seven hundred thousand villages of that subcontinent. A school was set up, sanitation was improved, the village council form of government from ancient times in India was revived, and health measures were taken, especially in improving the water supply. Even more important, some progress was made in improving the lot of the "untouchables" in the village.

Many people in other parts of the world were interested in Shantipur and the other Indian villages where reconstruction was going on. Ceresole tried to keep them informed about the progress in these "pilot projects" in village improvement. Because he could not write to all his friends and supporters individually, he started a series of printed letters which were later published in three books.

These letters reveal much about this prophet of peace, for they tell of his reading, his companions on shipboard, his meetings with Gandhi and other Indian leaders, his interest in the flowers and animals of India, and his reactions to the missionaries and the British officials in India.

Sometimes he had to adapt himself to local conditions and omit much of the hard physical labor which was such an essential part of the movement. But most of the time he would work all day alongside the local people and foreign volunteers. Then in the evening he would find different ways of relaxing. In one of his letters he speaks of sitting in his little hut "meditating like some hermit on mathematics or physics—a wonderful relaxation in any case. I had with me," he writes, "Eddington's second popular book and a recent volume of

Reichenbach on the Computation of Probabilities." To most of us that would not seem like relaxation, but to the former mathematics professor this was fun.

Many of the missionaries did not impress him. They kept too much apart from the natives and did too much preaching and not enough practicing of Christian service. To his friends he wrote, "Christianity should be concerned here not chiefly with its own 'success' . . . but in serving, and with the life of those to whom it appeals. It should have an infinite care for what these people are or have already, and that spiritual modesty which makes one ready to discover even a superior truth, perhaps just where one had come prepared to teach."

Gandhi impressed him deeply but Ceresole was not always in agreement with him. In another letter he says, "Without swallowing blindly all they say, one must listen and meditate attentively with a constant effort at objectivity, respect and affection, to persons like Mahatma Gandhi. . . ." Commenting another time upon this great figure, Ceresole said, "I do not think it is particularly by mental brilliancy that Mahatma Gandhi shines. It is rather by an inward force—whatever name one may give to it—which would enable one to count on him in any serious matter calling for sacrifice, in fact in the great and complex adventure of life. With Gandhi there is faith . . . a faith not found in the same degree in the mere politician."

His thoughts were not always on such lofty things, however. Ceresole was a great lover of nature and his letters often referred to the flowers, to the scenery, or to the peacocks, parrots, monkeys, and elephants he saw on his trips around India. In one letter he said that he went to sleep "lulled by the night breeze rustling through the palm leaves and the rhythmic sighing of the waves breaking on the shore. To awake here at dawn was as wonderful as to fall asleep by starlight." He wrote, too, of seeing "parrots and monkeys gravely seated four or five together, grouped at equal distances, ambling away without haste as the carriage approached" and of "the peacock in its wild state, spreading its tail half across the road, walking with slow paces as if in a courtyard and holding high its head crowned with aigrettes."

In his travels around India to see various projects for improving the village life of the three hundred million persons who lived in tiny hamlets, he took time to see the great shrines and places of beauty, such as the Taj Mahal. Of it and the Alpine scenery, he said, "Such things are not paintable! After having decided that the Taj at a distance of twenty yards seems even more truly inspired than at a distance of four hundred yards, one comes to the same conclusion when one examines its detail at a distance of twenty inches. . . . The greatest homage one can render to this monument is just this surprise."

Just before he left India in 1937 he prepared a statement for the newspapers which summarized in its first paragraph his ideas on peace. It read in part, "Peace is essentially not something negative, not simply the absence of war. Among other positive things, Peace requires that we should recognize good will wherever it is and not only in our own nation, race, class, party, or religion. The best way to have good will recognized is to get people of various nations, races, classes, religions, and parties to join in common work and service for an aim which every intelligent and sincere person agrees to be of supreme importance. Such is the work started now in different directions and by different groups for the help of the Indian villagers in their present distressed condition."

There were many tributes to Ceresole and his practical idealism. One spoke of the Service Civil International as "an oasis in the arid desert of warring Europe" and praised the members of it as persons "to whom humanity at large is but one family and to whom service of their fellow men is the keynote of their existence."

Of Ceresole himself one paper reported, "He is a living example of a yogi (saint) of modern times, not a politician, but something greater. Tall in stature, he is taller still in ideas and ideals and a fountain of inspiration for service and sacrifice."

Meanwhile events were taking place in Europe which would culminate in World War II. Being a keen observer of political affairs, Ceresole saw the storm clouds on the horizon and did what he could to alter the course of events.

He made a trip to Nazi Germany to see for himself whether the people there really wanted war or whether it was the government which was moving them in that direction. He made another trip to Italy and tried to persuade Mussolini to make use of the idea of the work camp for the employment of the thousands of unemployed Italian youth in a constructive service to their country.

War had broken out meanwhile in Spain and so the Service Civil International turned its attention to the suffering in that country. Their main concern was for the evacuation of children from Madrid.

When World War II broke out, Ceresole was utterly dejected. He had seen the results of World War I and he feared that the violence, destruction, and deaths would be even greater in this second international conflict. Within his own country he did everything possible to insure Swiss neutrality. In every conceivable way he encouraged efforts to mediate the war. Among other things he called upon Swiss munitions makers not to produce weapons and sell them abroad.

But this was not enough. He felt that he must cross the border between Switzerland and Germany to speak to responsible Germans. To do so legally was impossible. But that did not stop him. He knew the territory at the border well and was able to cross it without being stopped. His purpose was to talk frankly with German officials about the war and the treatment of Jews. It is doubtful if he felt that his words would do much good, but he felt compelled to act in this way, leaving no stone unturned which he could touch.

Once over the border he was caught and imprisoned. Returning to Switzerland, he was again imprisoned by the officials of his own country for having crossed the border illegally.

These two imprisonments and a later term of three months for failure to obey Swiss wartime measures seriously impaired his health. In the spring of 1945 he returned to his small cottage on Lake Geneva near Lausanne a sick man.

Throughout his life Ceresole had been a bachelor. But in 1941 he had married a friend whom he had known well since childhood, Lise David. Lise was a distant cousin and considerably younger than Pierre but their friendship had ripened over the years until they had decided to marry.

It was Lise who took care of him so lovingly in these last few months of his life. Friends came from all over Switzerland and from other countries to see him either in the tiny cottage or out on the porch, surrounded by flowers and over-looking the lake which he loved so much.

Then, on the evening of October 23, 1945, he passed quietly on to the next world.

Pierre Ceresole stands out among his contemporaries like the giant Matterhorn mountain stands above the peaks of his native Switzerland. He was a man with a sensitive conscience, a conscience which did not make life easy for him. It forced him to do things which others were not willing to do. He was a pioneer for peace, always out on the frontiers where most people did not dare to go until someone had showed them the way.

The prominent French writer Romain Rolland once said that Ceresole was "one of the great consciences of the Swiss. Such consciences save humanity." He might well have sub-stituted the word "world" for "Swiss."

Perhaps the most remarkable thing which Ceresole did was to develop the idea of peaceful service to humanity as an alternative or replacement for military service. Today that idea has caught on and thousands of young people have volunteered for such work. When the United Nations Educa-tional, Scientific, and Cultural Organization was founded, it approved this idea as an especially promising practice in pro-moting international understanding and it organized an asso-ciation of the various groups now sponsoring international work camps. Through this idea the life work of Pierre Ceresole is destined to continue.

Undoubtedly his greatest characteristic was his courage. In one of the 120 little black notebooks in his home, notebooks which he carried with him wherever he went in order to jot down his thoughts, one finds this comment written one day while working in one of his international work camps: "Fear—the principal enemy—especially fear of oneself. Fear of not being adequate, of repeating the same mistakes indefinitely. The greatest danger is compromise with the enemy within oneself.

"Fear of letting go of one's money.

"Fear of stepping out of one's environment.

"Fear of changing jobs.

"Fear of seeing things as they are.

"Fear of names, systems, words.

"Fear of death."

Ceresole was not without fear, but he had overcome most of his own fears. One of his chief characteristics was his courage.

He was likewise a seeker after truth. In his little notebooks are many pithy comments on this topic. One was, "This man will not lie—he is dangerous." Another, "Truth first—bitter pill, hard to swallow at times, but the only universal and infallible remedy."

He was a great lover of nature, too. He was able to enjoy fully the beauty of his native land and to see beauty in many common scenes around him. What is more, he had the ability to describe it simply and poetically. Another phrase from his notebooks reveals this in two sentences. He wrote, "Unbelievable beauty of God and of the morning! Snow in bloom on the mountains above and cherry trees in bloom down below." Even in the prison cell he was able to find beauty as evidenced by this statement, "Joy . . . joy . . . the oh so joyful cry of the swallows tracing the great curves of their flight, at top speed, in front of the prison windows. . . . Do you know anything more admirable, more expressive of freedom, courage, enthusiasm, the intoxication of energy, of the progress which does not come of itself but by the effort of the breast flinging itself against the air, in full flight, and of the muscles, securely tied to a bone built according to the calculations of the Eternal himself!"

Pierre Ceresole did not lead an easy life. His conscience did not permit him. But he led an adventurous life and towards the close of it he penned these words: "In spite of everything, the world is marvelous."

Here was a man who pioneered for peace, who made a distinctive contribution towards the creation of a world community based on peace and justice—a Quaker whose home was the world.

MAHATMA GANDHI

Prophet of Non-Violence

January 30, 1948, was a memorable day in Indian history and may well become an important day in the history of the world. Prime Minister Nehru has said that "a thousand years from now men will be thinking and talking about this day."

And the reason? It was in the evening of January 30, 1948,

that Mohandas K. Gandhi was shot by a young Indian fanatic as Gandhi was making his way slowly through the crowd which had gathered in the Birla House garden in New Delhi to worship with him in his usual evening prayer service.

It took only a moment and three shots from a pistol hidden in the young man's hand to kill Gandhi. Within a half hour the famous Indian was dead.

And within a half hour the whole world had heard the shocking news of his assassination. Millions of Indians of every faith and political creed were stunned by the passing of Gandhi. Countless millions in every part of the world joined in mourning the passing of this great Indian leader.

People differed in their estimates as to the reasons for his greatness, but everyone knew that a great world figure was gone.

At the time of his death newspapers and newsreels in every country carried pictures of the "Mahatma," or "Great Soul," as he was usually called. But these pictures were misleading. When one looked at them, all he saw was a homely little man with a tiny, close-shaved head, big ears, and a pair of thick-lensed glasses resting on a large nose. Or one saw a small, almost shriveled-looking brown figure with a homespun loin cloth wrapped around part of his body and a pair of sandals covering his thin, bony feet.

The papers and films also showed pictures of his possessions —and they were very few. There were the loin cloths and sandals, the glasses and a few books, a watch, some bowls for eating, and a few miscellaneous items such as the tiny statue of the three monkeys—"hear no evil, see no evil, speak no evil." That was all he owned, for he believed that the more possessions a person had, the less likely he would be to understand the poor people around him.

By the usual standards of the Western world this man had not been a success. In fact Winston Churchill had once called him a "half-naked fakir," and many had agreed with this blunt characterization.

Yet these same newspapers and newsreels spoke of Gandhi with great respect and even admiration. In their tributes they were joined by political leaders, religious leaders, and millions of common men and women from all over the globe. These people pointed out that this curious little man had defied the mighty British Empire and had finally won independence for India. They praised his efforts to remove the scourge of untouchability from Indian life and spoke of his success in having this practice outlawed by the new Indian Constitution. They pointed with pride to his activities in improving the standards of living in the seven hundred thousand villages of India. They explained how much he had done to emancipate women in that huge subcontinent. And they lauded his attempts to reconcile the Hindus and Moslems in their bitter fratricide at the time of the partition of India and Pakistan.

What it was that made this seemingly insignificant man so very significant is difficult to determine, but it is a question worth exploring. To find the answers one needs to study the growth of Gandhi from a shy boy in a small town in India to the assured leader of India's masses in his later life. It is a complicated story, covering nearly eighty years, but it is a tale well worth telling.

The story opens in the town of Porbander in western India, part way between Bombay and Karachi, on October 2, 1869.

It was there that Mohandas was born, the sixth child in the family of Kaba Gandhi.

Kaba was an important man in that town and section of India, serving for some years as Prime Minister. But what Mohandas remembered about him was the fact that he was patriotic to his clan, truthful, brave, and incorruptible. In his *Autobiography* Gandhi also mentions that his father was a bit short-tempered.

In that same book, Gandhi says that his chief remembrance of his mother was one of saintliness. She was a devout Hindu, painstaking in the celebration of holidays and in fasting. As a small boy Mohandas used to watch the sky with care, for his mother often vowed not to eat until the sun appeared, and he would long for the sun to come from behind the clouds so that the fasting would be over. His mother was also a woman of good common sense and seems to have been well informed on what was going on in her small world.

Neither of his parents was educated in the narrow sense of that word. In fact, Gandhi's father probably never went beyond what we would call the fifth grade. But he was a man of above-average ability, educated in the school of experience.

When Mohandas was about seven years old, his father became a member of the Rajasthanik Court, a very influential body which settled disputes between chiefs and their clansmen. This meant that the family had to move to Rajkot, where Mohandas was sent to school. In that respect he was lucky, for very few Indian boys and girls went to school in those days. In fact, even today more than 80 per cent of the people of India cannot read or write, although one should not confuse illiteracy with ignorance.

As a pupil Mohandas was not outstanding. He read his books, learned his lessons, and kept out of trouble, but that was about all. Years later he remembered that "it was with some difficulty that I got through the multiplication tables." His classmates remembered him as a skinny, shy little boy who came at the last minute in the morning and hurried off home at the close of the day, avoiding them most of the time.

The biggest event in those early years was his marriage at the age of thirteen to a little girl named Kasturba, who was only eleven. Of course Mohandas did not choose her. In fact he had not seen her since they were children back in Porbandar. The parents of these two had decided years before that their children would marry, and so the ceremony took place and Kasturba came to live with the Gandhis. This was a child marriage in conformity with the ancient customs of India, but it was a lifelong marriage which was later based on love and companionship.

Like most boys of his age, Mohandas was at times a young rebel. Eating meat was strictly forbidden in the Gandhi home, as in the homes of all good Hindus. Mohandas learned, however, that the older boys were breaking the law and were eating meat. At first he refused to join them. But when they pointed out that the English were strong because they ate meat, he thought he would try it. The result was an upset stomach and a nightmare. This deterred him for a time, but later he sneaked off to a restaurant quite frequently to dine on the forbidden meat. Then he decided that he could not indulge in this practice and gave it up.

He tried smoking on the sly, too, for a while. But again he decided to give up the practice. Basically he was an extremely honest person and it was the fact that he must conceal these things from his parents which really deterred him.

These early years passed rapidly and Mohandas was soon ready for college. At least, he thought he was. But the college authorities weren't so sure and at the end of the first semester they decided that he hadn't done well enough to remain.

Such was the story of his early life—and not too promising a story, either. Then, somehow, he began to wake up. Just what the events were which caused his awakening one cannot say definitely. One of them may have been his failure to make good in college. Another was probably the birth of a son to Kasturba and Mohandas's realization that he was now a father, responsible for a small family. In addition, his father had died and he was now more on his own than before.

The suggestion was made that he go to England and study to be a lawyer. That appealed to Mohandas, and Kasturba encouraged him, too. What better occupation for a young man than the law, especially when the best chances professionally for native Indians were as civil servants under the British?

There were strong objections, however, from the ruling men of Gandhi's caste. According to tradition, no Hindu crossed the ocean and mixed with non-Hindus. They forbade Gandhi's going.

But he went anyhow. In September 1887 he sailed for England, docking at Southampton. There he changed into his white suit and prepared himself for the trip to London. The white suit, however, made him conspicuous, and he learned for the first time how different this new country really was. People dressed differently, ate differently, lived differently. His international education was already under way.

66

Like most young people he did not want to be different, so he soon began studying speech, violin, dancing, and French. He bought a suit of Bond Street clothes, had his hair cut in the English style, and learned to tie a tie. Of course his meager budget suffered and eventually he decided it would be better to be himself—to dress and act like an Indian instead of an Englishman. Once he was clear on this point, he settled down to an intensive study of the law and to the cultivation of a few friends, most of whom he met in the vegetarian restaurant where he usually ate.

Among these friends in London were two English Theosophists and a Christian. Gandhi had not troubled himself much with religion up to this point; he had claimed for several years that he was an atheist. His Theosophist friends persuaded him to help them in the reading of the sacred writings of India. In doing so, he himself became interested in the great litera-ture of his country, especially the Bhagavad-Gita, one of the holy scriptures of the Hindus. Gandhi struggled through the entire Bible which his Christian friend gave him and was not impressed with the Old Testament. But the New Testament, and especially the Sermon on the Mount, impressed him deeply.

His philosophical education was largely laid aside, however, because of his desire to complete the examinations for the bar. He studied hard and on June 10, 1891, passed his exams. On the eleventh he was enrolled in the High Court, and on the twelfth he sailed for India.

Upon arriving home he received a terrific shock. His mother had died recently and the family had withheld the news until he had completed his exams and had returned to his homeland.

In India Gandhi tried to establish himself as a lawyer, first in Bombay and then in Rajkot, but he was only partially successful. An offer of a job with a Moslem firm in South Africa intrigued him and in the spring of 1893 he set off for his new post. He expected to stay about a year; actually he was to remain nearly twenty years. His life up to this point had been merely prologue. In South Africa he was to find the basic themes which would be woven into the symphony of his entire later life.

As soon as he arrived in South Africa Gandhi began his education in "second-class citizenship." Visiting the courts in Durban, he was asked to remove his turban. But the turban is considered a part of an Indian's clothing, and Gandhi refused. When the magistrate insisted, Gandhi removed himself from the court. In his *Autobiography* he records the significant statement, "My turban stayed with me practically until the end of my stay in South Africa."

Then, on the train trip to Pretoria, where he was to work, he was further instructed in the ways of this comparatively new land. Riding in the first-class section, he was accosted by the conductor and told to move to the third-class carriage. He refused. The conductor pled with him to act as other Indians acted, but he would not give in. As a result the police were called at the next station and Gandhi was thrown off the train. That night he stayed in a dingy, cold station, wrapped up in a light overcoat.

These and other events burned themselves into Gandhi's soul. At first he was angry, but his anger soon turned into a resolve to do something about the condition of his fellow Indians.

Soon Gandhi had organized the Natal Indian Congress and had become its secretary. From now on his fellow countrymen had a champion in South Africa. Attempts to deprive them of their right to vote would be fought. Injustices would be brought to court for possible redress. The Indians would be urged to educate themselves, to improve their sanitation, to forget their caste differences—and to raise their heads as free men and women.

To many people these were merely slogans, impossible ideals. But to Gandhi they became important goals, achievable goals if people were patient and persistent.

There were many battles ahead, but they were to be fought with new weapons. Some were to be fought with pen and type —through the pages of a newspaper called *Indian Opinion,* which Gandhi edited in English and Gujarati, the language of his province in India. Some were to be fought with spades and shovels and brooms, as Gandhi realized the importance of sanitation and hard work in the ghettos in which his people lived.

But the most important weapon of all was to be *Satyagraha.* There is no way of translating that word accurately into English. The nearest one can come to the idea behind the word is soul-force or truth-force. Sometimes people translate it as nonviolent resistance or civil disobedience. Perhaps a simpler way of stating it would be to call it a method of "striking— peacefully."

Gandhi had not originated the idea, but he was the first person in the world to use it as a political weapon on a large scale. No one knows how he conceived the idea of using *Satyagraha* in South Africa, but we do know from his own accounts that he had been reading and thinking a great deal in those early years in South Africa. He had turned again to the Bhagavad-Gita and the New Testament Sermon on the Mount. Then he had come across the writings of the great Russian author Tolstoi, especially a little book of his called *The Kingdom of God Is Within You*. Another book which touched him deeply was Ruskin's *Unto this Last*, which stressed the fact that the good of any individual is related to the good of all, that the work of every man is equally important if done well, and that the life of labor is the life worth living. To these should also be added Thoreau's "Essay on Civil Disobedience." And to the books should be added the important influence of several religious-minded persons of various faiths with whom Gandhi came into contact.

All these ideas churned about in his mind until he had developed his philosophy of life—a philosophy of service rather than self-interest, of justice for all rather than the self-aggrandizement of a few, of peaceful resistance rather than violence. It had taken Gandhi many years to arrive at these conclusions, but he was now clear in his own mind. With the certainty of deep conviction, he was ready for whatever might come. Gandhi would keep on growing as long as he lived, but his basic principles were settled.

His first use of *Satyagraha* came in 1906. It was late in the fall when the South African Government announced that all Indians must register with the government, give minute details on themselves, and be fingerprinted. In return they were to receive a registration card to be carried at all times in case they were stopped by the police. This was obviously discrimination of the worst sort. Only Indians were to be subjected to these harsh laws.

A meeting was called immediately and a huge audience appeared. The Indians were incensed over the new laws, but baffled as to what to do about them. Speakers inveighed against them in the Hindi, Tamil, Telugu, and Gujarati languages. They counseled resistance, violence, warfare. When Gandhi rose to speak, a wave of silence swept over the hall. The question on everyone's mind was what their leader would propose. He proposed resistance, disobedience—but of a passive or non-violent type.

When he had finished his talk, a member of the audience rose and suggested that they all take a solemn oath never to submit. Quiet reigned again. Then to a person they all rose and uttered in unison, "We swear in the name of the Everlasting God . . ." No name had been given to such resistance, but the word *Satyagraha* was the term decided upon later.

Within a few days the reports on registration came in. Only 511 out of 13,000 Indians had complied with the ruling. The others had refused to register. Gandhi and other leaders were arrested, but the non-resistance movement continued for months and years. And in 1913 it spread from the Transvaal into the Natal region when a law was passed making the marriages of Moslems and Hindus illegal. This was a ruse by which all children became illegitimate and unable to inherit property. In this way it was hoped that the Indians would be forced to leave South Africa.

As a protest against this new act nearly 4000 followers of *Satyagraha* started a march across the border from Natal into the Transvaal, headed for the Tolstoi Farm which Gandhi had set up for "displaced persons." This was clearly in defiance of the government, which did not permit such migrations in

South Africa. At the border they were met by the police and all of them were arrested.

But the prisons were not big enough to hold them all and the expense to the government was too great to hold them long. Furthermore, public opinion had begun to form on Gandhi's side. So a Royal Commission was eventually set up and in the spring of 1914 the Asiatic Relief Bill was passed, repealing the poll tax on Indians, making Indian marriages legal, and guaranteeing more rights for the Indians in South Africa.

Satyagraha had succeeded.

Now Gandhi was ready to return to India with his family, which by this time numbered four. In a few months another and longer chapter in his life would begin. The struggle would be greater and success slower, but again *Satyagraha* would be the chief weapon.

Back in India Gandhi spent several months traveling in order to get acquainted again with his native land. One of the first places he visited was Santiniketan (House of Peace), the international center in Bengal founded by Tagore, the great Indian poet. These two great men, who were to remain lifelong friends, discussed many problems together during the months that Gandhi, his family, and his followers spent with Tagore.

Then Gandhi started an ashram or settlement similar to the Tolstoi Farm which he had founded in South Africa. Scarcely had he gotten this project under way when a family of untouchables applied for admission. Gandhi gathered the twenty-five people who made up the small colony and asked for their decision. To accept the lowly applicants would be revolutionary, but these men and women were imbued with Gandhi's ideals and they consented. Soon after the untouchables arrived, contributions to the upkeep of the Farm dwindled and it looked as if it would be forced to close. But within a few days a wealthy Moslem drove by and donated enough to keep the community going for two years. He was unknown to Gandhi, but Gandhi was well known to him and this was his way of supporting the efforts to remove untouchability from Indian life.

Soon others began to show their interest in his various causes. Not the least among these was Jawaharlal Nehru, the son of a wealthy and distinguished Brahmin lawyer, who became one of his most important followers and later the man on whom Gandhi's mantle of leadership was to rest. But Nehru was but one of many thousands, and later millions, who began to look to Gandhi for leadership in their efforts to achieve justice and freedom after nearly two hundred years of British rule.

It was to these millions of India's masses that Gandhi appealed in 1919 when the British issued their famous or infamous Rowlatt Report, permitting British officials to arrest anyone taking part in seditious acts, "seditious" being defined as anyone disturbing the peace by speeches, marching in parades, or writing in magazines and newspapers. Up to the time of this report Gandhi had been a loyal British subject. He had supported the British in the Boer War in South Africa by doing ambulance work and in World War I. But he could no longer remain loyal. This was too much. From now on he would work for Indian independence.

By foot, by cart, by railroad third class he crisscrossed the country explaining his views and his methods. Eventually he intended to reach Delhi. But he was arrested before he reached that city. He was detained in prison only a short time and then released. But the people were excited and not all of them were convinced of the value of his non-violent methods. A group of mill workers even killed a police sergeant and that was too much for Gandhi. He started to fast for three days as a form of penitence, a way of telling people that he felt guilty for their crime. He even went so far as to call off the *Satyagraha* campaign.

But the people did not all respond to his pleas. Rioting continued and violence was frequent. The British became alarmed and when one of them, General Dyer, heard that a crowd of twenty thousand Hindus and Moslems were celebrating their festivals in the city of Amritsar, he lost his head. Without investigating why they had gathered, he dispatched his troops to the spot. Then a terrible massacre began. When the firing had stopped nearly fourteen hundred Indians had been killed and nearly twelve hundred wounded. To make matters worse an order was issued forbidding anyone to bury the dead. Insults of all kinds were added to injuries.

Finally the Congress Party, the group in India fighting for independence, decided to hold its meeting in Amritsar. Many of its leaders wanted to avenge the massacre, but Gandhi counseled patience. He pled with them to wait until they had seen whether England would punish Dyer.

When he learned that they would not, he issued one of his most famous statements. "No Indian," he said, "has co-operated with the British Government more than I, but when you approve the Punjab atrocities, I must revolt against you. You leave me no choice. My religion forbids me to bear any ill will towards you. I would not raise my hand against you even if I had the power. I expect to conquer you only by my suffering."

Such a strange statement for one man to issue in the year 1920. Another milestone in his life had been passed. From now on he would devote himself completely to the cause of Indian independence. From this point on he allied himself closely with the Congress Party and they with him. At their regular meeting in December 1920 they launched a program of non-co-operation which included the boycott of English schools and colleges, of courts and elections, of English cloth, and the eradication of untouchability in India. This last item was particularly momentous for it was the first such public statement in Indian history—and was due solely to the influence of Gandhi upon members of the Congress Party.

Part of the genius of Gandhi was his ability to understand the poor and illiterate masses of his country and to find symbols which they could understand. Two such symbols now came into use at his suggestion. One was the spinning wheel or charkha. This tool provided work for the peasants and substitutes for the foreign cloth which was now boycotted. And it served as a symbol of non-violent resistance to the British. Along with the charkha was the khadi or homespun cloth which people wore. This, too, served as a symbol, for it was easy to identify those who wore homespun. Gandhi himself added to the popularity of these symbols by spinning every day and by substituting homespun clothes for the foreign suits which he had previously worn.

The boycott of the British swept like prairie fire across India. Millions took part in it—women as well as men, Moslems as well as Hindus. In August of 1921 a huge bonfire of British cloth on the beach at Bombay dramatized the movement in the same way that the Boston Tea Party dramatized the American colonist's protests in 1773.

Then Gandhi pressed harder toward his goals. He urged the people to stop paying taxes, since taxes keep governments in power. But before this phase of the battle had started, riots again broke out and Gandhi decided that the civil disobedience campaign must end. India was not ready yet for such methods to be used.

So far the British had largely ignored the leader in this war against them. Now they focused their attention on him, arresting him for seditious acts. And one of the most curious trials of all history took place, curious because Gandhi had these words to say when he was asked if he were guilty: "Your honor, you know I am guilty. What else can you do but sentence me? I think you should give me the hardest sentence possible."

How ridiculous, some may say. But Gandhi thought differently. He realized that he had transgressed the British law. Legally he was guilty. Beyond that, however, he felt that there was a higher power—the rights of humanity. He had carried on his campaign with this higher power in mind and his people had misunderstood him. In a way, then, he felt responsible for the rioting and was willing to atone for their sins.

The sentence was for six years. For two of those six years Gandhi was in prison. Then he was released after a serious siege of appendicitis and an operation.

While he was recuperating, word came to him of riots and bloodshed between the Moslems and Hindus. Independence was one of his goals, but peace between the various religious groups of India was another. He gave a great deal of thought

76

to ways of stopping this bloodshed. Finally he decided upon a twenty-one-day fast. To his friends and followers this sounded like certain death. But he would not be dissuaded.

All India waited breathlessly for news and in the meantime the riots quieted down. At last the twenty-one days passed and Gandhi still lived. It seemed like a miracle for a man fifty-four years old and still recovering from a serious operation.

By 1929 the Congress Party decided that it was time to declare its independence. So it drafted a document very similar in its Preamble to the American Declaration of Independence, and set January 26, 1930, as Independence Day. To dramatize this event Gandhi decided upon a symbolic move. This time it was salt. In a country where the average income is far below fifty dollars a year per person, the tiny tax on salt seemed exhorbitant. From it England collected twenty million dollars a year, which was a huge figure.

In March of 1930 Gandhi and a small band of his followers started on a famous 200-mile march to the sea from his ashram, or settlement. Once they arrived there, and in the presence of thousands of other Indians, Gandhi walked along the beach and touched the sea, dipped a little bowl into the water, and returned to the beach to boil the water until there was only a small salt deposit left. This was another symbol of revolt, another signal for all India to stop paying the tax.

And India spread the signal up and down the land. England of course retaliated. Gandhi was imprisoned and within a few months nearly ninety thousand men, women, and children were thrown into prisons. All the leading members of the Congress Party were imprisoned and their meetings were held in prison. Attempts were made to get Gandhi to compromise, but he would not yield. Finally, on January 26, 1931, he was released.

The appointment of a new Viceroy for India, Lord Irwin, did result in some progress for the independence movement and Gandhi called off the civil disobedience campaign. Indians were allowed to make their own salt from that time on, the prisoners were freed, and some of the confiscated property of farmers were restored. Gandhi sailed for London to discuss English-Indian affairs, but the conference made little progress and another campaign was started against the government as soon as he returned to India. Gandhi was again imprisoned.

This time the English made a new move. They offered to give the untouchables of India separate elections. Gandhi wanted them to vote, but not in separate elections, which would further ostracize them from their countrymen.

This time he decided upon a fast unto death. And death it might well have been for this man of nearly sixty-three years if his followers and the British government had not agreed upon a plan for the untouchables to vote in the regular elections with other Hindus. Thus his fast had won a real victory.

It was one thing to secure equality for the untouchables in elections. It was quite another thing to wipe out evil practices which had persisted for centuries in India. The reports which Gandhi received in prison regarding the treatment of untouchables by the higher castes disturbed him and again he decided upon a twenty-one-day fast. Government officials this time were convinced that he could not possibly live. They did not want to be held responsible to India for the death of Gandhi, so they released him from prison. All India watched the daily bulletins, wondering how he could live. But he did live despite those twenty-one days without any sustenance except water.

Finally, when he had again recovered his health, he announced plans for his retirement. He would not return as expected to the ashram which he had established upon his return from South Africa. He would walk from village to village, talking to the people, instructing them in the methods of civil disobedience, urging them to help the untouchables and helping the untouchables to help themselves. Then in a few months he established a new ashram in the Central Provinces which he called Sevagram (Place of Service). The site chosen was a small village near the town Wardha and typical of the hundreds of thousands of tiny hamlets throughout India. Here Gandhi established a model community with a small hospital, a dairy, and a school. This would be the pattern for the reconstruction of village life throughout the entire subcontinent. There he would train young people to take part in a nationwide movement for village reconstruction. To this cause he gave much of his time and effort and thought in the remaining years of his life.

Meanwhile England had granted a small measure of independence to India through the India Act of 1935 and Gandhi, Nehru, and the other leaders had agreed to the terms of the new arrangement.

And then came World War II. England expected India to support her in this conflict, but Gandhi and the other leaders refused unless India was granted her independence. A deadlock resulted. Neither side would budge. Finally the Congress Party held a special meeting at which Gandhi spoke. He called upon them to use every effort which was non-violent to tie up the nation. "Quit India" became the battle cry of the embittered Indians.

The campaign caught on quickly all over India. But again there were those who used violent methods to accomplish their aims. Gandhi was distressed. To him independence was a cherished dream, but it must be accomplished without violence and bloodshed. The means people used were fully as important as the ends they sought to achieve. Good means must be used to achieve good ends. So, at the age of seventy-four, he began another of his famous twenty-one-day fasts. He grew weaker and weaker, but the English would not give in this time. He won the fast but he won no concessions.

Then within two weeks of the end of this fast a really tragic event took place in prison. Kasturba, who had been in jail with him as she had been on several previous occasions, fell by his bedside from a heart attack. For days Bapu, as he was sometimes called, watched at the bedside of Ba, as she was often affectionately referred to. On February 22, 1944, this faithful, loving wife, who had stood by Gandhi through all these turmoils and struggles and had given him great strength and courage to go on, passed away.

The days passed slowly now as he served his time in prison. Soon he was stricken with malaria and in May 1944 he was released "for medical reasons."

There was better news ahead, however. At the close of the war the Labor Party came to power in England, and the Indians knew that that was good for them. The new Prime Minister, Clement Atlee, issued a statement that India would be given independence and that the people of India would decide upon their own form of government.

How wonderful it would have been if India after all those years could have achieved her independence as a united nation, and peacefully. But it was not to be so. Riots broke out between Hindus and Moslems over Moslem demands for a separate country of Pakistan.

Gandhi was grieved. Was a divided India what he had fought all these years to achieve? Yet it was better to have two nations than a gruesome civil war. So he finally agreed to partition.

Many people feared that it would not be possible for Hindus to live in Pakistan or for Moslems to live in India. So Moslem families quickly gathered their possessions together and set out for Pakistan, and Hindu families set out for India. Millions of refugees crowded the roads and railroads.

What was there that Gandhi could do? He had just returned to Calcutta from a walking tour in Bengal on a peace march. Wherever he had gone the troubles between Hindus and Moslems had been quieted. Perhaps he could bring peace throughout the country by what he called "self-suffering," demonstrated by a fast of penitence. So he started fasting and within five days the people quieted down. Hindus and Moslems respected him and understood this way of talking to them. He was calling for peace and they obeyed. On the sixth day a deputation of Hindus, Moslems, and Sikhs came to him and promised to work together.

That was on the seventeenth of January, 1948. By the thirtieth he was able to walk in the garden of the Birla Estate where he was resting, and to take part in the evening prayer service which hundreds came to attend.

Then came the fateful event which removed the great Gandhi from India and from the earth.

He had been great during his life; he will probably be even

greater after his death. He is not an easy person for Westerners to understand for he was a product of India and the Orient. But he probably achieved greater victories for humanity than any other man in these times. He helped to free more than forty million untouchables from their slavery. He raised the position of women in India. He helped to win independence for more than four hundred million men, women, and children. He helped to show the way for the reconstruction of life in more than seven hundred thousand Indian villages. He experimented with a new method of action, through *Satyagraha*. He worked hard for better understanding between the various religious groups in his native land.

He was an ardent nationalist, but he was also an internationalist. As he saw it the two were not mutually exclusive. "My idea of nationalism," he once said, "is that my country may become free, that if need be the whole of the country may die so that the human race may live. There is no room for race hatred here. Let that be our nationalism." And upon another occasion he had this to say: "It is not nationalism that is evil, it is the narrowness, selfishness, exclusiveness which is the bane of modern nations which is evil. Each wants to profit at the expense of, and rise on, the ruin of the other. Indian nationalism has struck a different path. It wants to organize itself or to find full self-expression for the benefit and service of humanity. . . . For me patriotism is the same as humanity. I am patriotic because I am human and humane."

Truly he was a rare individual, one of the first among the citizens of the world.

TOYOHIKO KAGAWA

Practicing Christian

On Christmas eve of 1909 a Japanese student zig-zagged his way through the crowds of people loitering in the streets of the slums of Kobe, Japan. In his hands he clutched the few possessions that he owned. As he moved along, he stopped here and there to talk with a factory worker, a jinrikisha-puller, a beggar, or a gambler. He knew many of these people personally, for he had been visiting in this section of the city often during the past few months.

Now he had come at the age of twenty-one to live in the slums of Shinkawa, in Kobe. He was not forced by circumstances to do this; he had made the choice of his own free will. His neighbors would be the outcasts of society—murderers, thieves, prostitutes, cargo-carriers, fortunetellers, and day laborers. His home, like theirs, would be a 6-by-6-foot "cell," opening on a narrow, filthy, unpaved alley.

Sanitation was a meaningless word to his neighbors. They had common toilets, common kitchens, and no sewage. Many of them had diseases, such as tuberculosis, syphilis, and trachoma.

People did not live here—they merely existed. No one could really live in such filth and disease. They passed their days and nights in these slums, adding one meaningless day to another

85

until death claimed their weary bodies and warped minds.

Toyohiko Kagawa wandered through the crowds of men and women and children until he came to his new "home." It was a narrow room which no one else would rent. A murder had been committed there, and it was considered bad luck to move into such a place.

Why would a young man voluntarily move into such slums? Toyohiko had been driven there by his conscience. He had been preaching to these people for several months, but he soon realized that to be effective he must live among them and raise their sights rather than coming to them from time to time to talk to them about bettering themselves.

How he felt about them is expressed in this statement of his: "God dwells among the lowliest of men. He sits on the dust heap among the prison convicts. With the juvenile delinquents He stands at the door, begging bread. He throngs with the beggars at the place of alms. He is among the sick. He stands in line with the unemployed in front of the free unemployment bureaus. . . . I am fond of men. The worst, most fear-inspiring, demonized murderer somewhere in his make-up has that which is irresistible." That was the philosophy of life which drove him to the slums of Kobe.

He was only a young man when he began his work in the Shinkawa slums. But he was a mature young man with a passion for helping the outcasts of society.

He did not come as a dreamy idealist. He came as one who had known a life full of hardship and suffering and had discovered how to live above its petty annoyances and its painful trials.

Toyohiko Kagawa had been born in Kobe on July 10, 1888.

His father was politically prominent. He had been ruler over nineteen villages in the province of Awa, a pioneer in transportation in the port city of Kobe, and secretary to the Emperor's Privy Council. Much less was known about Toyohiko's mother. She was a geisha—a dancing girl who had given birth to Toyohiko out of wedlock. Later he was legally adopted, but the social stigma of illegitimacy stayed with him throughout his early life.

When he was four years old both his parents died and he was sent to Awa, an inland village where his father's legal wife and Toyohiko's foster grandmother lived. There he spent an unhappy youth, escaping the fury of his adopted mother by long walks along the river, visiting the imperial mausoleum, or wandering through the bamboo groves. Sometimes he rummaged among the family heirlooms stored away in closets and chests. He liked to play with the swords and armor of his samurai ancestors or sample the preserved plum pickles which former generations had stored away.

Another means of escape was in books. He was an avid reader and delved deep into the Chinese classics, the storehouse of Oriental culture.

At ten he became the head man of the territory, since he was then the oldest living male member of his family. But this was an honorary title and meant little to him.

Then there was work, and plenty of it. In the summer he worked in the rice fields or trod the human waterwheel to irrigate the fields. Sometimes he stood for long hours under the sun to pick the mulberry leaves on which the silkworms lived. In the fall he helped to harvest the rice and in the winter he helped to make sandals and garments out of the rice straw.

In both summer and winter he fished for lobsters, crabs, and shrimps to help supply the family table with food.

Eventually he was sent off to Tokushima to a boys' school. There he continued his unhappy existence. He had developed a sensitive soul and he rebelled against the crudity and coarseness of life in the dormitory.

Then one day as he was ambling down the street he heard music coming from a tent. He peered in and saw a group of boys and girls having a good time. He entered cautiously and stayed to hear Dr. Logan, a missionary, give a short talk.

This was the beginning of a friendship with the Logans and the Myers, missionary families. Both welcomed him into their homes. There he found good friends, good books, good music, good food, and good conversation. He soon joined the Bible study group of Dr. Myers and eventually became a Christian.

This change of religion infuriated his family. He was disowned and disinherited. From then on the Myers became his foster parents. Through them he entered Meiji Gakuin, the Presbyterian college in Tokyo, in 1905.

His hunger for learning was insatiable. He pored over Kant's *Critique of Pure Reason*, Goethe's *Faust*, Mueller's *Sacred Books of the East*, Darwin's *Origin of the Species*, and scores of other difficult books. Occasionally he embarrassed his professors with his knowledge.

But he was not just a theorist. He began to apply in real life the lessons he had learned in books. A beggar that he met along the highway became his roommate. The inhabitants of the slums became companions of his free time. In the college literary society he championed socialistic ideas and in the midst of the Russo-Japanese war he opposed Japan's participation. By reading Tolstoi and the New Testament he had come to believe that war was wrong and he would not take part in it.

Life was too strenuous for him and he contracted tuberculosis in his second year in college. For a year he had a "rendezvous with death" in an isolated seaside village. Life was full of agony and pain, but he poured himself out in deeds of kindness to the villagers, trying to forget himself and his troubles by helping others.

Paper was scarce and expensive, but he did find some old magazines around the village. On them he painted in Japanese style his autobiography, *Across the Deadline*. Eventually this story sold in over three hundred editions and was translated into several foreign languages. But that was not until years later. At the time of his illness it was merely an outlet for his troubled mind.

Finally he decided that "illness is a matter of the spirit." "I feel," he said, "that it is half mental and half physical. If you believe, come what may, you can overcome it and recover. That is religion. I have peace because my heart is easy. I have crossed the deadline so nothing matters. Since I have as good as died once, the rest is all gain. What is living to me is merely the spirit."

Once he had won a victory over the spirit, he seemed to win a victory over his body, too. He returned to Tokyo to complete his training at the Theological Seminary of Meiji Gakuin.

Then he became embroiled in trouble and it looked for a time as if he would not be allowed to complete his college career. A dispute had arisen between two faculty members, and one of them had been dismissed. Some of the students thought that the discharged professor had been wronged, so they started a strike. Many of the faculty members were disgusted by such action and five students were slated for dismissal. This action was announced at the regular chapel exercises, and the students involved were asked to come to the platform to shake hands with the president as a part of the ceremony of departure.

When Kagawa's turn came, he did not put out his hand for the farewell clasp. He took the president by the hand and said to the students and faculty, "Christianity is a religion of love. A school of love should guide a mistaken student. As God never abandons anyone, so a seminary ought never to drive a student away. Please forgive and reinstate the other four students and let the sentence of expulsion fall upon me alone."

The faculty did reconsider its action and all the students were reinstated.

Not many months after his graduation from Meiji Gakuin, he made the decision to go to the slums to live. He had not lived there long before he began to acquire a household of "guests."

His first "guest" was an alcoholic whom he renamed "Copper Statue." Next came a former murderer. Then a man without a job and therefore without food came to live with him. The money Kagawa had to live on was very limited, but he found ways to support this group of four. By cleaning chimneys he earned a little additional money. And by diluting the rice soup and limiting meals to two a day, the foursome lived on ten dollars a month.

The sights Kagawa saw and the people he met challenged him greatly. Sometimes it seemed as if he could not carry out his resolve to live in these slums. In such a period of despondency he wrote these lines:

One month in the slums,
  And I am sad,
    So sad
I am devil-possessed
  Or mad.

I came to bring
God to the slums,
  But I am dumb,
    Dismayed.
    Betrayed
    By those
Whom I would aid.
  Pressed down:
    So sad
    I fear
That I am mad.

Yet he managed to recover from such periods. In better spirit he wrote:

Farewell to paper-pasted walls
I get me up
And shove my shoddy sandals on.

Throughout this land
I go to preach,
"The Kingdom is at hand."

In the slums he visited the sick, wrote letters for the illiterate, gave advice when it was sought, adopted street waifs, preached on street corners, held Sunday School in vacant lots, and taught classes for children and adults whenever they could come. He was a one-man community center, a one-man church.

As he saw it, "The slums are a laboratory of life and human

society. From one point of view, I am doing research work with the slums as my laboratory and man as my major. Some people think of me as administering palliative remedies, but I am an industrious scientist. I am researching life at one of its outbreakings in the social order."

After five years of such research he was convinced that "one individual working for individuals cannot change society." He decided that poverty was the taproot of society's evils and that he would devote himself to raising the standard of living of Japanese laborers.

As he expressed it later in life, he was standing at the foot of the precipice, picking up people who had been hurled over the rocks. Now he wanted to see how one could have those people *before* they even reached the precipice.

He gathered together the results of his "research" in the slums of Kobe and published them in a book entitled *The Psychology of Poverty*. Then he left the slums, temporarily.

He set off for the United States and for Princeton University. His chief aim was to study the causes of poverty and ways of raising the standard of living for the people with whom he had worked during these past few years.

At Princeton he set himself to study with the same fervor with which he had always worked. On the side he served as a butler in New York homes, to earn part of his way. Finally, in 1915, he received the degree of Bachelor of Divinity from Princeton.

The next year he acted as secretary of the Japanese Community Association in Ogden, Utah. A major part of his work there was to settle labor disputes between Japanese and American tenant farmers and the farm owners.

In 1917 he returned to the slums of Kobe. "This time," he says, "I changed my technique. I began to organize labor unions and co-operatives. Unless there was a change in economic systems, I thought, it was completely hopeless to combat the slums."

In rapid succession he started the first labor school in Osaka, organized the first consumer co-operative among laborers, and founded the West Japan Branch of the Japanese Federation of Labor. Soon he helped to organize the Tokyo and East Japan branches of that same organization.

Of course there was opposition—bitter opposition, influential opposition, violent opposition. In 1921 the police declared labor unions unlawful. The laborers responded by organizing a strong nationwide labor union.

What they demanded was the recognition of the right to organize and to negotiate with their employers. They drafted a manifesto which stated their demands in these words:

Laborers are personalities. They are not commodities to be bought and sold according to a scale of wages based on the market price. Furthermore, they must be given the right to organize. For this reason we who belong to the army of producers make the following proclamation:

We are not machines. In order to develop our own individualities, to personalize society, and to secure the social order which will provide the producers a real culture, and give them security as to their livelihood, we demand the right to regulate our own circumstances.

Their demands were not met. And so thirty thousand of them went on strike. Kagawa had counseled against striking and had urged that all possible methods of mediation and negotiation be used.

But he finally joined in the strike and was imprisoned with several other leaders. Prison walls did not stop his activities, however. He used the thirteen days in prison to outline in his mind a novel, published later under the title *Listening to the Voice in the Wall.*

And while he was in prison another book of his appeared, called *The Shooter at the Sun*. It was read immediately by thousands of his followers and by other thousands who wondered what ideas were in the head of a man who would challenge the industrial leaders of their island.

After his release he continued to help organize the laborers. It was his hope that these labor unions would be different from those in other parts of the world. "The blind aping of imported ideas regarding labor unions," he said, "will never save the day. For Japanese workers there is a Japanese way. That is invention and creation. Intelligently, accurately swing your hammer and watch the results. Unions are necessary but labor problems can be solved only by the inner awakening of the laborer. There is but one course for the laborers. That is production motivated by love."

Then in 1924–25 he visited England in order to study the principles and practices of the Labor Party, which was then in control under the leadership of Prime Minister MacDonald.

When he returned to Japan he started a similar party. Labor needed to speak through legislation, he maintained. And the only way in Japan was through a separate labor party.

In 1925 the right of the laborer to organize was finally recognized. This recognition was largely the result of the work of

Kagawa. Group action was making progress where individual action had largely failed.

But this was only one right which he felt the laborer rightfully had. There were others. He spoke of "the laborer's right to labor, freedom of domicile, an opportunity to round out their personalities, freedom of marriage, freedom of migration, recreational privileges, liberty of speech, the right to organize, the right of associational contract, and of religious freedom."

Today those rights seem pretty obvious to most Americans. But it must be remembered that Kagawa was living in Japan and the date was the mid-twenties. Japan had industrialized quickly but in many ways she was still living in a semifeudal state.

The laborer was not the only forgotten man in Japan, however. Kagawa knew that well. Of equal importance was the peasant farmer. The population of Japan was growing rapidly and there was little land to cultivate. Farmers tilled small plots of ground, usually consisting of one to three acres. Often it was hilly land and had to be terraced. In addition, his tools were primitive. On top of all these hardships was the fact that many of these peasants had to share their scanty crops with absentee landlords.

As a result many of the farmers and their families drifted to the cities. Sometimes they found work and often they did not. Or they found work for only part of the year—and at ridiculously low wages. Very often the city was like quicksand and they became caught in it, gradually sucked under by the terrific pull of poverty and crime.

Kagawa saw that something must be done. Japan needed food desperately. She needed to learn how to raise more food on the barren, rocky hillsides. She needed to learn how to find more food in the sea.

And she needed to help keep people on the land. There he felt that people could lead "the good life" better. Working in the soil did something worth while to people. "This civilization of steel and concrete separates mankind from the soil," he often said. "The soil is God's footstool. The scent of the soil heals men. They ought to live close to it."

Such thinking caused him to organize the first farmer's union in 1921 and to start a magazine called *The Soil and Freedom*. The program of this movement was as broad as the laborers' had been. It had as its goals better housing and sanitation, more scientific agriculture, education for everyone, and the formation of co-operatives of all kinds. All this was to be accomplished by peaceful means—by evolution rather than by revolution.

Kagawa has always had the knack of picking up simple but important methods to promote his ideas. In that respect he is like Gandhi. Reading a book one day by the prominent American geographer J. Russell Smith, he came across an idea which was particularly appropriate to Japan.

This was the idea of planting nut trees on the sides of the mountains. The trees would stop erosion and thus save the precious soil of Japan. They could be planted on hitherto unproductive ground and save the really productive land for vegetables and grain and other products which demand better soil. And the nuts from these trees could provide much needed protein food for the people or inexpensive feed for chickens.

So Kagawa began growing nut trees on small experimental plots of ground. He and his friends planted walnuts, oaks, and pecans. They soon found that pine trees could also be used for the same purposes.

Another idea was to encourage the farmers to raise goats on the sides of the mountains and on other rocky or poor land.

Still another idea was to establish whaling stations in the waters of southern Japan, similar to those already in existence in the northern waters. Kagawa pointed out that the meat of one whale equals that of a thousand pigs, not to mention the much needed oil that can be obtained from them. As he saw it, the Pacific Ocean could become "a pasture for whales."

In a similar way much more use could be made of the various seaweeds to help the Japanese to obtain more food and better balanced diets.

Most of these ideas were new and they had to be "sold" to the public. Kagawa had learned by now that he could write and that thousands of people would read his novels. Why not include these ideas in a novel.

So he started to sell Japan such ideas through popular books. In *A Grain of Wheat*, for example, his hero starts a co-operative enterprise in nut trees on the side of the mountain near his native village. The story was a simple one but it sold widely and people began to talk about these ideas all over Japan. This was a novel means of popular education.

Even more important to him was the co-operative movement. In it he saw a chance for people to work together and to control their own businesses, a chance for the profits of work to be shared among those who produced wealth in various forms. To him co-operatives were the Christian way of doing business. They were "Christianity in action," as he repeatedly said.

97

In such enterprises co-operation would replace competition and people could learn the art of living together, studying together, playing together, and making decisions together.

Everywhere he went he urged the establishment of co-operatives of all kinds. There were to be consumer co-operatives, producer co-operatives, marketing co-operatives, credit unions, insurance co-operatives, and mutual aid societies.

Realizing that Japan is Tokyo-minded, he started his first consumer co-operatives in five Tokyo universities and he opened the first medical co-operative in the same city. Then he began co-operative schools for training leaders in this movement.

Quite rapidly the movement spread to other large cities and then into smaller towns and into the country. These new forms of economic activity soon attracted the attention of the Communists. For a time they attempted to dominate them, reshaping them to their own purposes. But Kagawa fought vigorously and tirelessly against their becoming Communist-dominated or even Communist-influenced. He was most anxious for these to be motivated by Christian principles rather than Communist ideology. In the end he was successful.

Meanwhile he was also fighting for universal manhood suffrage. And in this fight, also, he was a winner. Japan gave the right to vote to all men, even though it was not yet ready to give it to women.

Because of all these activities, and several more which have not been mentioned, Kagawa was looked upon by the government as a dangerous radical. He was always stirring up trouble, always starting something new. He was continually making people dissatisfied with the status quo.

Then something happened which changed the minds of even the conservative governmental leaders—at least for a little while. On September 1, 1923, came the terrible Japanese earthquake. Two thirds of Tokyo was destroyed and most of Yokohama was laid waste. Over a hundred thousand persons were killed and six billion dollars' worth of property was destroyed.

To cope with this emergency a National Economic Commission was appointed. Kagawa was appointed to that important body. That was the beginning of a short-lived connection with the government as an adviser on social and economic questions. The country's leaders knew that he was brilliant and imaginative. They knew, too, that millions admired and respected him. They needed him.

Soon after that he was asked to serve on the Commission on Unemployment, Labor Exchanges, and Emigration. Eventually he was asked to take charge of the social work in Tokyo. He accepted the job but refused the $9000 salary. Ten days a month he devoted to this work and he was able to bring about a complete reorganization of the Bureau of Social Work. As part of his work he was able to start a slum clearance program in the five largest cities of Japan. Included in this was a project in the Kobe slums where he had worked so many years.

He was also able to assist the thousands of families who lived on houseboats. For them he provided visiting nurses and dormitories for the younger children. For those in dire distress he helped to provide burial funds. In key centers of population he set up new social settlement houses. And for the unemployed he arranged municipal employment bureaus.

All this had been accomplished when Japan was in the throes of the world-wide depression. But when the darkest days of that depression were over, he gave up his post to devote himself to his many projects for bettering the life of the Japanese people.

Over the years he had become convinced that numbers count. He had learned that the impact of a large group of people is more powerful than that of a small group. What would happen in Japan if a million men and women would become Christians and really practice their religion daily?

This question called for action. So he started in the early thirties on a campaign to win a million converts to Christianity. It was to be interdenominational with everyone taking part. Missionaries and ministers were to be included, but more important would be the lay leaders in this movement. To train such lay leaders he organized small, short-term schools. At the same time he began to supervise the publication of inexpensive newspapers, magazines, and books to be used in the movement. These were intended chiefly for factory workers and farmers.

Kagawa and his helpers were not able to win a million people, but he was able to report in 1936 that "there are twice as many Christians in Japan today as there were ten years ago."

By now the world had heard of Kagawa. They wanted to know him. They admired his practical idealism. They felt that he was really a practicing Christian. They wanted to hear him, see him, counsel with him, worship with him, be inspired by him.

So in 1931 and again in 1936 he toured the United States, traveling on to Europe. New Zealand, the Hawaiian Islands, and the Philippines called and in 1935 he visited them. In the early forties he made a trip to India.

Meanwhile the Japanese had invaded Manchuria and later China proper. What could a Japanese Christian say to that? With characteristic courage Kagawa spoke out against the action of his nation. He refused to sign a statement of leading Japanese Christians justifying the war as one of "self-defense." As a result he was imprisoned in August 1940 for violating the military code. After a few weeks' internment he was released.

In a short time came Pearl Harbor, and Japan was again embroiled in war. Communications with his friends in the United States were cut off. Broadcasts from him began to be beamed to this country and in them it seemed as if Kagawa had become an intense nationalist, supporting the war and defending Japanese actions. Some of his so-called friends began to fall away.

But those who were close to him knew better. He had led a delegation of twelve prominent Japanese Christians to the United States in 1936 to see what could be done to prevent the war which they thought was coming. They had known where he stood then and they were confident that he would not change his opinion—no matter what happened.

Then word began to come through neutral countries that he had been arrested by the Japanese government for writing a poem entitled "Tears," in which he decried the treatment of Chinese civilians by Japanese soldiers. Word came later that he had been arrested upon two other occasions. Obviously the broadcasts were being "doctored" for propaganda purposes.

When the war was over it was discovered that Kagawa had spent the last few months in hiding. He had taken to the woods when his friends warned him that he was to be executed as a traitor. For months he had subsisted on nuts, grasses, and tea made from bark. He was physically but a shadow of his former self.

With a new Liberal government in power in postwar Japan, Kagawa was again invited to counsel with the rulers. Even the Emperor wanted his advice, and Kagawa has been in almost continuous contact with him on both personal and practical matters of state. Many of his friends and fellow party members have been elected to the Diet or Japanese Congress and have been selected for posts in the Cabinet or in other positions of trust.

Kagawa has been urged to run for office or to accept several positions in the government, but he has always declined. There are other things to be done which he wants to do. There is the labor movement to assist, the co-operative movement to prod, the farmers to help. There are schools which need to be built and textbooks which need to be rewritten. These are the things he can do best. Others can make their contribution through politics.

Since the war there have been two movements to which he has given increased attention. One of these is the attempt to build a thousand rural centers throughout Japan. This is not a new idea, but it is the expansion on a large scale of an old dream. In each of these farming and fishing villages Kagawa wants to build a small chapel which will serve community life. In the daytime they will be used as day nurseries and in the evening as night schools for adults. On Sundays they will serve as places of public worship.

As heads of these rural centers he wants lay leaders and teachers, and he has already trained several hundred persons for such work. Each of these persons is to be trained in the

Bible, the history of Christian brotherhood, new methods of agriculture, and rural sociology.

Several of these centers are already functioning, and more are planned as soon as the money is found to build the chapels. After that the local groups will have to finance them.

Such is the dream for the revitalizing of rural life throughout Japan, a dream which is being translated gradually into reality. In many ways it is like the village reconstruction carried on by Gandhi in India.

The second movement to which Kagawa has devoted himself since World War II has been one for a federated world government. He has founded and is now chairman of the International Peace Association and has made himself personally responsible for the financial success of its monthly magazine, *World State*. He has also become vice-president of the Union for World Federal Government.

He was glad when the United Nations was formed in San Francisco, but he was disappointed that it did not develop more along the lines of a world government. To him that is the only hope on the political level. On the economic level he believes that there must eventually be an extension of the co-operative movement on a world scale if there is to be perpetual peace. Co-operation must replace competition in economics as well as in other phases of living.

These two themes were uppermost in his mind when he came again to the United States in 1950 and made a cross-country speaking tour. On that six-month trip he spoke 350 times to an estimated national audience of 350,000 persons.

To these listeners he often added another message in response to questions about the conflict between the United

States and the Union of Soviet Socialist Republics. To such queries he replied, "Russian Communism cannot compete with Christianity. Its only adherents can be those to whom *true* Christianity is unknown. . . . Until the people in the Christian countries accept Christ and his teachings their nations will not be free. Until the peoples who live unblessed by Christ can feel him present at their sides, they will continue to search, using violent and egocentric means, for some inkling of security."

Those were strong words, but most of his listeners could "take them" from Kagawa because they knew that all his life he had been practicing what he preached. They might not always agree with him, but they admired his tenacity and his courage. They knew that doctors had told him many times that a man whose body was filled with disease as his is could not continue to work so hard, to travel so much, to lead so many movements. But they knew, too, that he had kept on for many years against that advice. They knew that Toyohiko Kagawa was a man of courage, a man of indomitable will, a man of imagination, a man of purpose—a practical idealist, a practicing Christian.

FRIDTJOF NANSEN

Modern Viking

Nature seems to have done her best to make the Arctic and
the Antarctic forbidden territory. But there have been many
explorers who have dared to trespass on these vast stretches of
water, snow, and ice. Their names are familiar ones like
Amundsen, Byrd, Nansen, Shackleton, Stefansson, and Peary.
All of them were great explorers—great men.

But among them Fridtjof Nansen's name leads all the rest. He was a great scientist, a great geographer, and a great explorer. That is part of his claim to fame. But he did not stop with those accomplishments. He was also an explorer in better human relations and in better international relations. That is the other half of his greatness, and perhaps his more important claim to fame.

Yet there was little in his early life to indicate how famous he would become. He was born on October 10, 1861, at Fröen on the outskirts of Oslo, Norway. His parents were well to do, but they raised their children in Spartan simplicity.

Fridtjof's father was a lawyer and an industrious, gentle man. His mother was dynamic, intelligent, and individualistic. In later life he was able to combine the best traits of each of his parents and to draw strength from both of them.

As a boy he led an active, outdoor life. He swam and fished and hunted as most Norwegian boys do. He skied and skated and boated up and down the famous fiords of his native land. He was a good rifle shot and an accomplished yachtsman.

By the time he was seventeen he was the Norwegian skating champion and at nineteen he held the world's speed record on ice.

These sports appealed to him for their own sake, however, rather than as means to gain prizes and awards. In later years, speaking to the Educational Society at Oslo, he decried the new emphasis in sports. "Skiing," he told his audience, "has lost a part of its value, owing to the fact that the competitive spirit has been allowed to dominate. The goal of all manly exercise should be the building up and strengthening of body and soul, and it should at the same time lead us into the open.

But many of our sportsmen have become mere muscle machines—race horses—bending all their strength and energy towards making records and getting in a few meters ahead of their competitors."

Fridtjof liked to be alone as a boy, too. He would take camping trips into the woods or go on long hikes by himself. These times meant much to him and he said years later that "the solemn pine forest marked my soul for life." Speaking another time he urged people to seek solitude more often. "It is in the wilderness," he said, "in the solitude of the forest, within sight of the wide expanses, far from the madding crowd that character is formed. And it is men of character that our age needs." He could speak with authority, for his life had been shaped in part by such solitude.

As a boy Fridtjof had an artistic side, too. He liked to write poetry and he enjoyed painting pictures. He did not consider these hobbies "sissy." They were just as enjoyable as sports and he spent hours in both these activities.

His interest in science started early in life. The story is told of a trip to the Oslo Fair with his brother. Their parents had given them generous sums of money to spend on whatever they chose. Imagine their surprise when the boys returned home with tools! Their parents were afraid that they had missed some of the fun at the Fair, so they sent them back with more money. But again they came back with tools. Perhaps to please their parents, or perhaps to satisfy their "sweet teeth," they did spend a little money the second trip on cakes and candy.

There are also stories of chemical concoctions and experiments with clocks as well as good grades at school in science to prove the boy's early interest in science.

Fridtjof's real education, however, began at the age of twenty. He was studying zoology at the time and one of his professors suggested that Fridtjof go with him on a seal trip into the Arctic Ocean. There he could learn something about animals from first-hand experience.

So in March 1882 young Nansen set out on his first trip to the North. He was not a good sailor and was often miserably seasick. However, he was a good gunner and was put in charge of one of the sealing boats. There he began his apprenticeship in handling men, an experience in which he was highly successful. Years later one of his men could write of him, "As a leader he was a good companion, yet never lost the place of authority. He worked under the same conditions as his comrades, never spared himself or took special privileges, but worked harder than anyone else."

Probably he got his training for such later work on this trip to catch seal.

One thing baffled his companions on this sea voyage and that was the enormous amount of time he spent dissecting animals. He kept so busy hacking away at all kinds of creatures that one of the sailors commented that he would certainly make a good veterinarian someday!

Two discoveries on this trip stood out from all the rest. One was some driftwood. The other was some dirt. It was astonishing to find them in this land of ice and snow and Fridtjof thought about them a lot. He knew that pine trees grew in Norway, but from there could not have drifted so far north. He knew that Greenland and Iceland had no trees; therefore, the driftwood pine must have come from some place in Siberia. But how?

Nansen was not sure, so he took the specimens back to Norway. He kept on thinking about them and they had a decisive influence on his later life.

The Arctic had fascinated him. The ice had cast its spell over him. He would not escape the experiences of this trip throughout his life.

Upon his return home he was offered the job of curator of the natural history collection in the Bergen Museum. He was only twenty-one then, but he took it.

Curiously, he who had loved the outdoors was now to be confined indoors. He who had chosen zoology rather than physics or mathematics because it was less confining found himself shut up in a museum. But it was a real honor for one of his youth and inexperience.

Nansen confided in his diary that these years at Bergen were "lonely years." But they were certainly successful ones. He gained a good reputation as a scientist and was offered positions in several universities, including Yale and Indiana universities in the United States.

In 1886 he interrupted his work for a trip to Italy. There he studied at the new laboratory and aquarium in Naples and learned about the method which they were developing at Padua of making slides of the central nervous systems of animals. Laboratories and aquariums are commonplace today, but in the late nineteenth century they were attacked as "frills" in scientific education. Nansen's interest in these new facilities and his support of them helped in the establishment of a biological laboratory at Dröbak, Norway, in 1894. His study at Padua also aided him in the preparation of his doctoral dissertation, "The More Minute Structure of the Central Nervous System."

But Nansen could not forget those long white stretches of ice in Greenland. As he looked over that unknown, uncharted expanse on the map, he felt like Kipling's "Explorer":

> "Something hidden. Go and find it, Go and look behind the Ranges.
> Something lost behind the Ranges. Lost and waiting for you. Go!"

And he went. His scheme was a startling one. He proposed to land on the east coast of Greenland and work westward to the Danish settlements, making the crossing by skis. Most people thought it was a foolish idea. All the successful expeditions had started from the west. How did he know that all of Greenland was covered with snow and ice? What would the expedition do when they left the sealing vessel on the east coast and had nothing to return to?

The university approved the trip but the government rejected it. Just as he was about to give up hope, a Copenhagen merchant sent him 5000 kroner to finance the trip.

On June 4, 1888, together with three more Norwegians and two Laplanders, Fridtjof Nansen set off from Iceland on a sealer. Painstaking effort had gone into the preparations. Nansen, for example, had slept in the mountains night after night, experimenting with sleeping bags of various kinds until he was certain that reindeer skin was the best material for this purpose, considering its weight and its warmth. He had designed and built sledges which could be fitted together and equipped with sails. He had planned everything, down to the minutest detail, even including red silk veils to protect the men's faces against the penetrating rays of the sun.

A week later they caught sight of Greenland. All night they fought the wind, rain, and ice. When they were almost there, the boat was torn open by ice and before it could be mended the ice had closed in and was too rough to pass over. Six weeks elapsed before they could navigate the ice-blocked fifty-mile passage to shore.

Meanwhile the current was moving south, carrying them with it. Finally on July 29 they reached land. But they were three hundred miles south of their intended landing. There was a settlement about two hundred miles away to which they could have retreated. But with Nansen in command there was to be no retreat.

Instead, they headed the boat north, living on dry bread, dried meat, and cold water, dodging icebergs and the terrible waves created when ice broke off the glaciers and dropped into the water.

On August 10 they landed on the eastern coast of Greenland and in a few days they started over the land. It was not an easy trip. They had to go up glaciers and over bare rocks. Part of the time they had to push or pull their heavily loaded sledges.

By August 22 they had reached the top of the mountain rim and could see the giant icecap stretching before them. The snow was like sand now and difficult to cross. The wind was blowing against them.

Then Nansen changed their route in order to make the wind an ally rather than an enemy. Traveling was hard enough, even with the wind behind them. Nevertheless, they pushed on.

There were compensations, however, in their enjoyment of the free Arctic shows each night—the northern lights. Nansen has described them: "When the ever changing aurora borealis danced light and fairylike over the southern sky, perhaps in more radiant splendor here than anywhere else in the world, it was possible to forget our trials and tribulations. Or when the moon came up and followed its silent course across the star-strewn heavens, played over the tops of the ice ridges, and bathed the whole of this stark world of ice in its silvery rays—then peace descended all about us and life became beauty."

On September 24 they set foot on bare ground again and by October 3 they had arrived at the settlement of Godthaab on the western coast of Greenland.

They had crossed this vast country by ski and sledge and had proved that its interior was an unbroken icecap covered with deep snow. They had recorded temperatures, wind currents, heights and depths of snow, and many other climatic conditions of the interior which greatly affected large parts of the northern hemisphere.

There was plenty of time to write up these discoveries, for the last boat of the season had left for Norway two months before their arrival. They must spend the winter in Godthaab.

Nansen used the time to advantage. During these days of confinement he wrote the first draft of a book, *The First Crossing of Greenland*.

When that was done, he turned to the writing of another book, *Eskimo Life*. This was his first experience with primitive people and he was shocked. This is what he reported in his book: "When we brought them [the Eskimos] Christianity and the products of our civilization, they were forced to recognize us as their masters and since then they have been steadily deteriorating. Every time I saw one of these people suffering from or falling a victim to the vices that we brought them, the feeling of justice was awakened in me. . . . If that feeling of justice were fully alive among us, then we would all feel urged to put right the wrong." On his return to Norway he was to become a champion of the Eskimos—and later of other dis-tressed peoples.

The next spring they were able to get back home. On May 21, 1889, their expedition reached Copenhagen, Denmark, and on May 30, Oslo. In both cities they were received with enthusiastic demonstrations.

Once home, a new conquest awaited Nansen—and in an entirely different field. Out skiing one day, he spied a pair of skis jutting out from one snowdrift and a pair of ladies' boots from another. True scientist—or was it true male?—he investi-gated. In the snow he found Eva Sars. Eva was an accomplished singer, the daughter of a well-known zoologist and explorer. Soon she was the wife of another zoologist and explorer—Fridtjof Nansen.

For their honeymoon they went on a lecture tour of Europe. It closed in Stockholm, where Nansen was awarded the famous Swedish prize, the Vega Medal, for his Greenland expedition.

During the next few years he served as curator of the zoologi-cal collection in the University of Oslo.

But he could not forget that driftwood and dirt found on his first trip north. One of his friends examined this material and proved that the moss and marine plants which they con-tained were like those found in the Bering Strait. To convince Nansen further that his theory was correct, a pair of oilskin pants, a list of books, and a list of provisions of an ill-fated expedition were found in Greenland three years after the expedition ship had been sunk while searching for a new passage through Bering Strait to the North Pole. A "throwing stick" like those used by the Alaskan Eskimos had also been found in Greenland.

It all seemed to add up to something. Nansen was pretty certain that the Arctic currents moved north from the Bering Strait towards the North Pole, and then south to Iceland and Greenland.

He wanted to test this theory. Why not build an ice-proof boat, "bum" a ride north on an ice floe across the North Pole, and then journey south to the large islands which were located to the north and west of Norway. At least it was worth trying.

Again he was discouraged by many leading explorers. One of them called the idea "Nansen's illogical scheme for self-destruction." But ridicule did not stop Nansen.

With the aid of a famous shipbuilder, a new type of vessel was constructed which could withstand the ice. It was made with rounded sides so that it could slip out of ice jams and rest "like a ball on a platter." It was strengthened with iron ends and oak and pine sides 24 to 28 inches thick.

This time the Norwegian Government, the King, and private individuals saw to it that the expedition was an all-Norwegian one, completely financed by them.

The odd-looking ship was christened *Fram*, which means "Forward." In June of 1893 it sailed out of Oslo harbor with Nansen and twelve companions on board. It made its way around the northern end of Norway, then headed northeast towards Siberia, skirting the northern coast of Europe all the way. It passed south of the island of Novaya Zemlya and into the dangerous Kara Sea.

There it encountered ice drifts and "surpassed our boldest

expectations." On and on it traveled until it passed the most northern point in Europe—Cape Chelyuskin. On September 22 the expedition reached the edge of the ice pack, pulled up the rudder and propeller, and made ready to drift for the next few months wherever the ice took them.

They were soon convinced that the boat was iceworthy. The worst possible fate that could overtake them was enforced idleness and boredom. But the party was well prepared for such an eventuality. In the provisions they had included a thousand books, many games, and musical instruments. Workshops were opened to make shoes, clothing, skis, sledges, kayaks, and tools. Observations were to be recorded of the water, the currents, marine life, and the heavens.

October passed, November, December, January. Finally September of 1894 rolled around. In a year they had drifted only four degrees north. Three of those had been within the first six months of their trip. At that rate it would take them seven or eight years to complete the voyage!

Nansen consulted the ship's commander. They agreed upon a dash to the Pole on skis. Six months later, on March 14, 1895, Nansen and Johansen, the best all-round athlete and skier in the group, started off together with three dog sledges, two kayaks, and twenty-eight dogs. Ahead of them lay a four-hundred-mile trip which they calculated would take fifty days.

They had not counted upon pressure ridges thirty feet high nor had they realized that the ice would drift south almost as fast as they could move north. On April 8, 1895, they reached 86° 14′ N.—almost two hundred miles nearer the North Pole than anyone else had ever reached.

But they were forced to turn back. They headed towards

Franz Josef Land, where they hoped to catch a boat back to Norway.

Then one night they forgot to wind their watches and their calculations as to their position were completely upset. Their negligence cost them months of hardship.

April passed, May, June; only three dogs remained. In his diary Nansen wrote, "No sign of land in any direction and no open water. We do not know where we are, and we do not know where this will end. Meanwhile our provisions are dwindling day by day." Luckily towards the end of the month they killed two seals and in July added some bear meat.

On July 24 they sighted land and dug themselves a hut 10 feet long, 6 feet wide, and 6 feet high. There they spent the next nine months. Rocks covered with bearskins served for beds, gauze bandages soaked in blubber for lights, an almanac for reading, and bear and walrus cooked in every possible way for their two meals a day.

These months were long, discouraging ones which tested the physical and mental endurance of both men. They could revel, though, in the beauty of the ice, floodlit by the northern lights.

Nansen longed to express the scene in music. Lacking that ability, he captured it in poetic prose: "Nothing more wonderfully beautiful can exist than the Arctic night. It is dreamland, painted in the imagination's most delicate tints. It is color etherealized. One shade melts into the other, so that you cannot tell where one ends and the other begins. And yet they are all there. No forms—it is all faint, dreamy color music, a faraway, long-drawn-out melody on muted strings. . . . Presently the aurora borealis shakes over the vault of heaven its veil of

118

glittering silver—changing now to yellow, now to green, now to red. It spreads, it contracts again, in restless change. Next it breaks into waving, many-folded bands of shining silver, over which shoot billows of glittering rays. And then the glory vanishes. Presently it shimmers in tongues of flame over the very zenith, and then again it shoots a bright ray right up from the horizon until the whole melts away in the moonlight and it is as though one heard the sigh of a departing spirit. Here and there are left a few wavering streamers of light, vague as a foreboding. They are the dust from the aurora's glittering cloak. . . . And all the time this utter stillness, impressive as the symphony of infinitude."

Finally, on May 19, 1896, Nansen and Johansen set out on their hazardous journey home. They traveled across crevasses hidden by snow, and through water thick with dangerous floating ice. To rest the dogs they often pulled the sledges themselves, wearing shoulders raw in the effort.

Then—on June 17—they heard a human voice! A voice and the barking of dogs. They cried out in indescribable joy. Imagine their surprise to find that it was Frederick Jackson, an English explorer, who had letters from Norway which he had brought the previous summer.

August 13, 1896, found them back in Vardö, a small fishing village in northern Norway. From there they flooded the country with telegrams to family, friends, and sponsors.

But what had happened in all these months to the *Fram*. Where was their ship and its crew?

During the time since Nansen and Johansen had seen it, it had floated faster than anyone had dared to dream. It had reached a point within fifty miles of the most northerly position that Nansen had reached. The crew had spent the previous winter directly north of Nansen's underground hut!

Nansen was thrilled to receive a telegram from them reading, "Skjaerve, Greenland, August 20, 1896. Fram arrived here today in good condition. All well on board. Leaving at once for Tromsö. Welcome home. Sverdrup."

When the expedition was reunited, they set out together for Oslo. Their journey down the coast was a triumphant tour all the way. "Wherever we passed," wrote Nansen, "the heart of the Norwegian people went out to us—from the steamers crowded with townsfolk in holiday attire and from the poorest fisherman alone in his boat among the skerries. It seemed almost as if old Mother Norway were proud of us, as if she pressed us into a close and warm embrace, and thanked us for what we had done. And what was it after all? We had only done our duty; we had simply accomplished the task we had undertaken, and it was we who owed her thanks for the right to sail under her flag. . . . I realized to the full for the first time how near this land and this people lay to my heart. If we had sent a single gleam of sunshine over their lives, these three years had not been wasted."

Awaiting them in the Oslo harbor were more than a hundred ships of every size and description. As they landed and made their way to the university and King's Palace, they were jubilantly received by a throng of proud Norwegians. Few of them understood the scientific importance of the expedition, but all of them thrilled to this great exploit of their countrymen.

Nansen and his men had proved that there was no land near the North Pole. They had shown the world a new way to explore. They had traced the course of the Gulf Stream under the ice. They had touched the northernmost point yet reached by man. They had assembled a mass of valuable scientific data.

Nansen spent the next four years recording these data in two volumes called *The Norwegian North Polar Expedition, 1893– 96*, and in a more popular book called *Farthest North*. This popular account was fittingly dedicated to his wife: "To her who christened the ship and had the courage to remain behind."

He was made a professor in the University of Oslo, but freed from teaching until this work was completed. In his absence the Nansen Fund for scientific research had been started and a marine laboratory and aquarium established in Oslo.

This was the climax of his career in exploration. He was only thirty-five, but he had accomplished more than most people do in a life twice that long.

There were short expeditions in the years that lay ahead, but a new role was waiting for him.

Since 1814 Norway had been a part of Sweden. It had been allowed to elect its own parliament and to levy its own taxes. Its foreign affairs, though, were still in the hands of the Swedish King.

Then, in 1885, the Swedish Constitution was revised and the Swedish Foreign Minister obtained power over Norwegian foreign policy. The rapid growth of Norwegian shipping and her free trade policy was opposed to Sweden's high tariff. This complicated an already tense situation, for the Norwegians were a proud people and wanted to be entirely free of foreign rule.

Tension between the two countries mounted and in 1905 Norway voted to separate from Sweden. Sweden was determined not to let her go. That might have meant war between them, with the rest of Europe eventually sucked in.

In this time of national crisis, Norway turned to Nansen. He was summoned to the capital. There the crisis was discussed by the men in power.

The next day Nansen was in Denmark consulting with the government officials. That evening he went on to England, where he stayed a month, interpreting Norway's position.

Eventually Norway gained her independence and the dispute which threatened the Scandinavian peninsula—and all of Europe—was peacefully settled.

To this brilliant chapter in world history Nansen had contributed greatly. The new and independent nation of Norway approached him to be King, or President, or Prime Minister. He declined all three positions. Finally he consented to be their first Ambassador to England, a post he held for a little over three years.

All through this national crisis Nansen had been planning an expedition to the South Pole. Then in January 1907 a fellow Norwegian named Roald Amundsen came to him with an offer to buy the *Fram*. The visitor proposed to take it to Bering Strait and drift, perhaps for seven years, eventually crossing the North Pole. The man was young, his plans were complete, and he was sincerely interested in exploration.

Should Nansen aid him? If he did, it meant abandoning his own South Pole expedition.

Amundsen suggested a compromise. He would accompany Nansen on a trip to the South Pole. After that, he would go to the Arctic. Nansen thought it unwise for anyone to spend so many years in the ice regions. In the end he agreed to sell the *Fram* to Amundsen. No one knows what prompted his decision, but it is thought that his wife greatly influenced him.

What we do know is that Nansen watched the *Fram* set out for the Antarctic on June 7, 1910, with Amundsen as its commander. For Nansen that was "the bitterest hour" of his life, the more so when Amundsen eventually became the first explorer to reach the South Pole.

Soon World War I commenced. Norway was trying to remain neutral in the early months. In order to live she had to sell, and Germany was her best customer for fish. To live she also had to buy food, and the United States was her best source of supply. In 1917 the United States entered the war and the export of food was almost stopped.

Norway was faced with starvation. Again she turned to Nansen. This time he was asked to head a commission to obtain more food from the U.S.A. The price the United States demanded was the cessation of Norway's shipments of fish to Germany. To comply would have meant war with Germany and would have laid Norway open to attack from this near neighbor.

A compromise agreement was worked out with Norway sending less fish to Germany and receiving more food from the United States. Famine was averted. Again the people were deeply indebted to Nansen.

He was appalled by the "nightmare of insanity" in Europe, as he called the World War. "If civilization is not to be destroyed," he said, "there must be no more war."

To him it seemed that the most promising way to stop war

was to organize a League of Nations. He worked untiringly to help establish that organization and to have it include the small neutral nations. When that goal was accomplished, he worked equally hard to persuade the Scandinavian nations to join.

Nansen felt that the League was a new "ship" that "sails a new course with the future hopes of mankind on board." It was right that he should be named Norway's first delegate to the Assembly of the League in 1920 and for ten successive years.

So closely was he associated with the League that one journalist said he was "one of the sights of Geneva—the proudest after Mont Blanc." He spent much of his time in the world capital and people were hopeful of the success of the organization when they saw this tall, slim man with prominent forehead, fair hair, blue eyes, weathered and wrinkled face, and stern mouth. They knew that he was pouring his life into the League and that he really wanted it to succeed, even if many others did not. They trusted him implicitly.

One of the most stupendous jobs which confronted this new body was the care of hundreds of thousands of war prisoners. Great numbers of them were in remote places like Siberia or Turkestan, dying of typhus, cholera, scurvy, malaria, or tuberculosis, or going insane from loneliness and loss of hope.

Many of them were declared free citizens at the close of the war, but they had no funds to travel or no means of transportation. Others could not return to their native lands because of political changes which had taken place there. They were stranded with no work, no food, no one to help them, and no hope. Some were so isolated that it was years before they even knew that the war had ended.

Who was to bring order out of such chaos? Who would be politically neutral in such a tense international situation? Who could command the respect of the whole world?

It was decided that Nansen was the man. He was offered the job and accepted. He felt that this might be an opportunity to bring prestige to the League and to promote international understanding.

The difficulties that confronted him were almost insurmountable. Russia was in a state of revolution and her transportation and communications were disrupted. Her government was considered an outlaw by many nations. She, in turn, would not co-operate with the League, because it had barred her from membership. The League had little power and no funds.

As usual there were those who said that nothing could be done. But they had said that about the polar expeditions, too. Nansen knew better. He decided to act as an agent of the individual nations rather than as an official of the League. That satisfied Russia. Despite chaotic conditions, the Bolsheviks supplied two transport trains a week. From England Nansen obtained ships which had been seized from Germany during the war. An international loan was obtained to support the project.

Within eighteen months nearly half a million men and women were returned to their homes. The health measures were so thorough that this was achieved without the spread of epidemics. It was a great victory for the League of Nations and for humanity.

Meanwhile thousands of Russians were fleeing from the Revolution. They did not know where they were going. They only knew that they must leave that country. Neighboring nations were already crowded and would not accept them. Unless someone helped, they would die by the hundreds and thousands.

At the same time the Turks had been victorious against the Greeks and were pushing them out of Anatolia and Thrace. Penniless and hungry, the refugees were streaming into Greece. Greece was not able to help these immigrants, even though they were fellow countrymen.

No voluntary organization was big enough or powerful enough to cope with this situation. It was obviously a case for the League.

Here was human driftwood tossing about on the turbulent waters of postwar Europe. Fridtjof Nansen had always been interested in driftwood—material or human. Perhaps he could salvage them.

Consequently, he was appointed High Commissioner for Refugees and set about saving human lives. Thousands of children and adults were admitted by Bulgaria, Czechoslovakia, France, Sweden, Palestine, the United States, and other countries.

In the Greco-Turkish trouble, a mass exchange of nationals was arranged and nearly two million persons were moved in the next eight years.

Out of this grew the famous Nansen passport. This was a piece of paper which identified the holder of it as a person who no longer had any nationality, but who had been registered with the refugee authorities. Such passports were issued to thousands of persons, and with such identification papers they could travel from country to country.

Even more tragic than these refugees were the victims of the Russian famine in 1921 and 1922. In the summer of 1921 the Volga River had dried up and the grain fields had been scorched and burned. Thirty million or more people were starving, eight million of them children. Would the League of Nations help?

Nansen championed their cause. But day after day a decision was postponed. Finally the matter was turned over to the Committee on Political Questions. They decided that private agencies should handle this enormous job.

Nansen then took the question to the Assembly of the League of Nations. There he pled earnestly and eloquently in his booming voice. He pointed out that "less than half of the cost of one battleship, the cost of maintaining only half a battalion of soldiers, would feed the starving of Russia."

The League listened to him and applauded loudly. Then they voted "No" to his request.

Individuals and organizations and a few governments, notably the United States, came to the aid of starving humanity. Under the direction of the Nansen Committee, the Hoover Committee, the Quakers, and others, millions of lives were saved. But the League had failed on this point and Nansen was tragically disappointed.

In 1922 the Norwegian Parliament honored his work by voting him the Nobel Peace Prize. Speaking on this occasion, the chairman of the Nobel Committee said of Nansen, "The most significant factor in the work we have before us is that it has delved deep into the primordial roots of human fellow-feeling which lie deeply buried in all of us—the feeling that the human race is one—however much it may split itself up into states and societies." After mentioning Nansen's Arctic exploits, he said, "A submerged current which few have had faith in has again borne Nansen forward—the deep current of human sympathy underlying the layer of ice which surrounds states and individuals in the struggles of the day and the trials of life. He had faith in that current and through that faith his work has triumphed."

In the few remaining years of his life Nansen continued to devote himself to international humanitarian work. In the League he upheld the World Court as another step forward in organizing the world. He fought successfully against the seizure of Corfu by Italy. He worked against making the mandated territories into colonies of the major powers. He favored Germany's entrance into the League as one way of making it a league of *all* nations.

He defended the small nations so vigorously that when the delegates came together for a new session, they would say, "Let's hope that Nansen hasn't discovered another nation since we last met."

Continuously he pressed for disarmament, realizing that "disarmament of the mind is more important then disarmament of the nations."

In May 1930 he died. His funeral was held on Norway's Constitution Day and attended by one hundred thousand people. To these men and women he personified the ideal Norwegian. To countless others he personified the ideal citizen of the world. He was both.

As he once said, "I see valleys and mountains, woods and

green meadows, fields where the golden grain stands ready to be cut. This glorious land is mine. I want to live, to give it my best powers. . . . I see farther ahead a new world to be built and I want to help build it."

He had certainly done his best on both counts.

JOHN BOYD ORR

World Hunger Fighter

You and I live "in a crazy world—a world of abysmal poverty with potential abundance within our reach." That is what Sir John Boyd Orr told the students of Glasgow University in Scotland in 1947.

And Sir John knew what he was talking about. At that time he was Director General of the Food and Agriculture Organization of the United Nations, and he had spent his entire life in studying the problems of food and people.

At the tip of his tongue were the startling facts uncovered in 1946 by a World Food Survey conducted by the FAO with the help of seventy nations. He could prove by facts that it was "a world of abysmal poverty" and he could prove by the results of nearly thirty years of research that "potential abundance [is] within our reach."

He knew, for example, that every person in the world needs at least 2550 to 2650 calories per day as a *minimum* for healthy living. He knew, too, that these calories should be well distributed among such foods as cereals, roots and tubers, sugar, fats, peas and beans, fruits and vegetables, meat, and milk.

But he knew that over half of the world's population existed on less than 2250 calories per day and that those calories were seldom well distributed. He also knew that less than one third

of the world's population had a reasonably good food intake of over 2750 calories, even though they were not always properly balanced.

"Think of it!" he often said. "A thousand million people in the world who have never had enough to eat—not only the famine-threatened millions, but all the other countless millions who, short of starvation, have never known what real health means. And a thousand million peasants and farmers in poverty because they can't produce the food the hungry need, or if they do, face ruin because of something called 'overproduction.'"

Furthermore, he was painfully aware of the fact that each year there are between twenty and twenty-five million more people in the world to feed.

These and other facts disturbed Sir John deeply. He wanted people everywhere to know about them. He wanted to arouse public opinion to do something about them. He was interested in a better world and felt strongly that "hunger is at the heart of the world's troubles." As he sometimes phrased it, "You can't build peace on empty stomachs."

But where had he gotten these ideas? you may ask. To answer that question we need to go back to his earlier life and trace his development from an ordinary Scotch lad to his later position as number one hunger fighter in the world.

His life began on September 23, 1880, in Kilmaurs in the Ayrshire country in Scotland. Appropriately enough, he was born on a farm.

His family was poor and as a boy he had to work hard to help supplement the small income which they had. He also had to help in order to educate his brothers and sisters, for the Orr family were great believers in education.

Completing his work in the local schools, he went off to the University of Glasgow to study for the Presbyterian ministry, as his two older brothers had done. During his college years he happened to take a course in zoology just to satisfy his curiosity about the theories of Darwin, which were becoming so popular in those days. That class changed the course of his life. He decided to become a scientist instead of a minister.

He completed the work for a master's degree in the arts, taught a few years, and then returned to his alma mater to work on two further degrees. The first of these was to be in medicine and the second in science.

It was about this time that Sir Frederick Gowland Hopkins discovered what we now call "vitamins" in the new scientific field of nutrition. Working in the hospitals of Glasgow as a young interne and in the slums of that city as a young doctor, Orr became intensely interested in this new field. He studied everything available and talked with everyone who knew anything about it.

Then in 1914 he was made director of a new institute for research in animal nutrition which was being set up in the cellar of Marischal College in Aberdeen.

But World War I interrupted his work. He was called up and spent the war years in the Royal Army Medical Corps and in the Navy. For bravery under fire he was given two medals—the Distinguished Service Order and the Military Cross.

After the Armistice, he returned to Aberdeen. There he began his explorations into ways of improving livestock and increasing crop production. The institute attracted nationwide and then world-wide attention for its findings. It grew and grew. Eventually it was named the Rowett Research Institute and included the thousand-acre Duthie Experimental Farm, the Walter Reed Library on nutrition, and the Strathcona Club, a residence hall for scientists who came from near and far to learn the latest in animal nutrition.

One of the most important undertakings of the Rowett Research Institute was the study of the land and cattle of two tribes in East Africa. Originally this mission was intended merely as a study of the effect of the poor pasture land on their herds. But Orr was interested in the effect of bad land and poor cattle on people, too. So he added doctors to the mission and asked them to study the comparative health of the two tribes whose lands and herds were being investigated. One of these tribes was a meat-eating and blood-drinking group. The other was a cereal-eating and milk-drinking tribe. This made the study ideal from a comparative point of view. The results of these studies added a great deal to the science of social medicine.

In 1925 Orr carried out a controlled test among school children in the seven largest towns in Scotland. To one group he gave a pint of milk a day at school. The other group were not given this extra amount of nourishment. As a result, the first group showed an average acceleration in the rate of growth of 20 per cent. The health of this "milk group" improved greatly, too.

Today this experiment would not need to be carried on, for people would know that the "milk group" would grow faster and be healthier. But in that period proof was needed. People had not been convinced of the differences in food value of various foods. They had to be shown.

Throughout the years at Aberdeen Orr had accumulated a

large amount of information, and in 1929 he decided to share this with a large public through a book. In *Minerals in Pastures and Their Relation to Animal Nutrition* he summarized the pioneer work of the Rowett Research Institute. Even though it was written a few years ago, it is still consulted as a classic in the field of animal nutrition.

Orr's thoughts were now primarily about human nutrition. As he tells it, "I can persuade farmers to take an interest in nutrition because I can prove to them that it pays dividends in terms of their stocks and herds. But I cannot get them interested in the nutrition of their own children, let alone the children of other people. Yet I can prove as a scientist and as a doctor that that would pay incomparably greater dividends."

Finally he hit upon the scheme of a nationwide inquiry into the relationship between the incomes of British families and their diet and health. Some of his friends warned him against such a survey. They said it was not wise to mix science and economics. But this did not deter Orr.

Early in the thirties he launched the survey and in 1934 he submitted his findings to the British Association for the Advancement of Science. His figures showed some astounding conditions. They showed that 50 per cent of the British people did not have an income which would buy an adequate diet. Lacking such a diet, they were in poor health. Malnutrition was the result of poverty.

The British people were shocked by this survey. It was issued just before a general election and became a political issue. Committees on malnutrition were organized and candidates were bombarded with questions as to what they intended to do about the national health.

People who lived in the cities began a battle to lower the price of food. They wanted lower prices on such important products as milk, dairy products, eggs, fruit, vegetables, and meats. It was true that this would lower the income of the farmers, but the nation's health was at stake.

Great Britain was aroused, and the result of public opinion on her food policy will be seen a little later when we come to a discussion of food rationing during the war. Let us return a moment to see what happened to Orr, the man who had caused this furore.

In 1935 the King knighted John Boyd Orr for his services to his country in the field of agriculture and nutrition. From then on he would be known popularly as Sir John—at least until 1949 when he was given another and higher title and was made a peer of the realm.

Meanwhile other responsibilities came to him. He became a member of the British Nutrition Committee, in addition to being a member of the Colonial Agriculture and Animal Health Council, on which he served twenty years, and chairman of the Scottish Scientific Advisory Committee, which advised the government on the health and welfare of the Scots.

The results of the research into human nutrition in Great Britain were widely distributed in other parts of the world. Similar research had been carried on in a few other countries in the 1920s and 1930s, particularly in the United States.

Meanwhile the Great Depression had spread around the world, especially in the industrialized countries of western Europe and the United States. More food was being raised than in previous years, but the prices were too high for people to purchase it. Wheat was being burned in the United States and coffee was being burned in Brazil. Australia could not sell its butter and Argentina could not dispose of its beef.

The Australian delegate to the League of Nations, Stanley Bruce (now Viscount Bruce), felt that something drastic should be done. He presented his concern to the League and two committees were appointed. One was asked to look into the question of defining the food needs of people all over the world from birth till death. That group was appointed in 1936 and Orr was made a member of it. The other committee of experts were asked to submit a report on the question of food as it related to agriculture, health, and economics.

Neither of these committees was likely to bring action—at least for many months or years. But the first step towards action had been taken. Facts were to be assembled and later publicized. More important, national governments were called upon to submit data and to study conditions in their own countries. Such fact-finding bodies were set up in more than twenty countries.

This was progress, no matter how slow. And much of the credit for this little bit of progress was due to Sir John. As soon as the League approved his proposal, Stanley Bruce and his co-worker Frank McDougall, both from Australia, sent a telegram to Orr in Scotland. It was adapted from the famous words of Bishop Latimer when at the stake in Oxford. It read, "Be of good cheer, Brother Orr, for we have this day lighted in Geneva such a candle, as by God's grace, shall never be put out."

Then came the invasion of Czechoslovakia and World War II. The League practically disappeared and the work of its food committees was forgotten. But the idea of better health through better food had caught on and there would be action elsewhere later.

During the war in Great Britain it looked for a time as if the food front would be as vulnerable, or more so, than the fighting front. Normally Britain imports two thirds of her food from abroad. More than half of her dairy products come from Europe, and especially Denmark. It would certainly take all the ingenuity of men like Sir John to provide her with food when countries like Denmark were occupied by the Nazis and shipping from abroad was so difficult and dangerous.

Yet at the end of the war the health standards of Great Britain had actually risen. She was healthier than before. For example, there were fewer deaths of babies at birth in 1942 than in any previous period of English history. Studies of the growth of children in England and Scotland showed that they had made greater gains than in prewar Great Britain.

Why? There is no easy answer, but here are some of the ways in which Great Britain managed to improve her health during the war.

Food production was increased by finding unused land for farming. Machinery was imported, largely from the United States, to replace workers. A Women's Land Army was organized to replace farm workers who were soldiers. Acting on the theory that there was no need to carry water across the Atlantic, dehydrated food was imported.

Furthermore, tax money was used to subsidize essential foods so that everyone could buy foods that really matter. Even more important, a strict and extensive rationing system was set up. In it special allocations were provided for children and expectant mothers. Factory canteens and British restaurants were also set up to serve meals at prices people could afford.

As a member of Churchill's Scientific Committee on Food Policy, Orr was helping to shape these plans. Behind the scenes he was helping to put into practice many of the ideas for feeding the British people which he had been preaching about so long.

As if this were not enough, he took on the direction of the North of Scotland College of Agriculture and the professorship of Agriculture at Aberdeen University. These were added duties, in addition to his regular work as Director of the Imperial Bureau of Animal Nutrition at Aberdeen and his editorship of *Nutrition Abstracts and Reviews*. In addition, he was an officer in the Home Guard. Quite enough for one man.

Orr was also looking ahead to the postwar world. This was not escape; this was good planning. As he saw it, the Allies would win the war quicker if they knew what they were fighting for and could attract others by the justice of their cause. So in 1943 he published a small book on *Food and People*. It was popularly written and filled with pictures and simple charts so that many people would read it.

He based the book on the theme of the Atlantic Charter, promising freedom from want to all men in all lands. To him, "Food is the first want or need of all men." In the book he spelled out how he thought this first need could be achieved in Great Britain and eventually in the entire world.

In the conclusion of the book he declared that if the recommendations were accepted whole-heartedly and "carried into effect with the same vigor with which the war is being waged, a new chapter in our civilization will be opened." In that case he saw the masses of mankind "developing to the full their inherited capacity for health and physical well-being, . . . an expansion of trade and industry, . . . and the increase in wealth more equally distributed than was the case following the Industrial Revolution."

Little did Sir John know that in a few years he would be selected to implement many of these ideas through the Food and Agriculture Organization of the United Nations. But he was ready for whatever might come. He had thought through his ideas. They were well seasoned by years of experimentation and experience.

Meanwhile he had made a trip in 1942 to the United States and had talked to nutritionists, agriculturalists, and politicians about the topics closest to his heart. Many of the seeds which he had sown on this trip were to grow and yield a good harvest in postwar conferences on food and people.

Returning to Scotland, he learned that his only son had been killed in action as a member of the Royal Air Force. This was another and very intimate lesson in the wastefulness of war. Later he would have more to say on this subject.

Early in the war Roosevelt had proclaimed the Four Freedoms as an ideal. All through the war Orr had been thinking of ways to implement them, once the war was over. Eventually he decided that he would start with the problem of food and agriculture. So while the war was still raging in both hemispheres, a conference was called at Hot Springs, Virginia, to discuss the establishment of a Food and Agriculture Organization. Orr was not there in person, but he slipped in in an unexpected way—like a shadow.

During those meetings a film was shown called "A World of Plenty." Towards the end of the film the face of Sir John

Boyd Orr appears and he speaks briefly but tersely on the problem of food for all. It is a stirring scene and the delegates were moved. They rose to their feet and applauded this world hunger fighter, even though he was not present. It was a minor point in their deliberations, but it was not soon forgotten.

Plans were made at this meeting for some kind of Food and Agriculture Organization and, after a lot of work by an Interim Commission, another meeting was called in October, 1945, in Quebec. In that historic city FAO was formally launched as the first specialized agency of the new United Nations. In fact, the UN as such had not yet been formed.

For its first Director General the organization chose Sir John Boyd Orr, the short, spry Scot with the shaggiest eyebrows in Great Britain and one of the wittiest tongues in the British Isles. They wanted a man with his passion for bettering the world; his experience as an agriculturalist, nutritionist, and scientist; and his persistence and ingenuity in working towards his goals.

Since the United Nations had not been formed, there was no oath for him to take. So he sat down and penned his own. In slightly revised form it is used today for everyone who works for the United Nations or any of its specialized agencies. This is the oath that Orr wrote for himself:

I solemnly undertake to exercise in all loyalty, discretion, and conscience the functions entrusted to me as a member of the international service of the Food and Agriculture Organization, to discharge those functions and regulate my conduct with the interests of the Organization only in view, and not to seek or accept instructions in regard to the performance of my duties from any government or other authority external to the Organization.

The program they gave him was general enough. It consisted of the following five points:

1. To help nations to raise their standards of living
2. To improve the nutrition of the peoples of all countries
3. To increase the efficiency of farming, forestry, and fisheries
4. To better the conditions of rural people
5. To widen the opportunities of all people for productive work by means of the four points above

To accomplish any one of these would cost millions of dollars. But the FAO was very modest when it went to the forty-two countries which were originally members. It asked only for $5,000,000, or less than it costs to clean the streets of New York City after one snowstorm.

Looking ahead for several years, Sir John saw the work of FAO shaping up into three major tasks. The first of these was immediate. FAO needed to help avert starvation in those parts of the world which had suffered from the war and from crop failures. The second was similar. It was to increase the regular production of food by stepping up the production of fertilizer and farm equipment. The third was a longer term proposition. It was to improve nutritional standards all over the world, but particularly in the less developed areas.

To assist in all this work, the FAO needed facts and more facts. So one of its first jobs was to assemble all the data that it was possible to collect on food around the world. That is what we referred to in the opening paragraphs of this chapter as the World Food Survey, the first contribution of FAO as an infant institution. Even though they were not all members of the organization, seventy nations submitted data for this first world-wide survey of food ever undertaken in human history.

The shortage of food in 1946 was acute, and the FAO knew that something must be done. So it called a Special Meeting on Urgent Food Problems in Washington, D.C. At this emergency conference twenty-two of the countries most concerned with food conditions made plans for using the 1946 harvest to the advantage of the most needy people and made plans for maximum production in 1947. They also decided upon quarterly reports to FAO on the food situation within their own boundaries so that others would know what the world situation was and would plan accordingly. To carry out these aims they set up a temporary International Emergency Food Council.

To stop at this point, however, would have been disastrous, for these measures were taken only for the short term. If FAO was to function properly, it must think about long term planning, too.

Sir John and the members of the FAO Secretariat therefore drafted some "Proposals for a World Food Board." These were submitted to the next yearly conference of the organization, held in Copenhagen, Denmark, in 1946. The main idea behind these proposals was to try to prevent the disastrous slumps which usually follow wars and to save non-perishable food in the good years so that there would be a reserve for the lean years. The plan was similar to the "ever normal granary" scheme which had already been put into operation in the United States in order to set aside grain in years when there was a surplus for years when there was a scarcity. It was hoped that these plans would help stabilize prices of the major agricultural products on the international market. According to the proposals, all this work would be carried on by a World Food Board.

When the delegates assembled in Copenhagen, they were divided in their reactions to these proposals. Among those who were opposed to the plan were the members of the United States delegation and those from Great Britain. According to them, too much power was being given to this new international organization. They feared the plan would cost too much. Some felt that it was socialistic.

The general ideas contained in Orr's proposals were approved, however, and a World Food Council was established. This council was not given the power or the funds which Orr had proposed, but it was given *advisory* power to urge governments to act along the lines it felt best. It was a compromise agreement, but it was better than nothing. So the World Food Council was approved and began to function within a few months.

There were many other ways of helping to improve the food supply of the world and of assisting in a more just distribution of what was produced. On their budget of $5,000,000 a year FAO was able to accomplish a wide variety of objectives. Here are a few of the things they did in the first few months.

During World War II Greece had suffered greatly. She was anxious to improve her agricultural production as rapidly and efficiently as possible. So she turned to the FAO. In 1946 a small group of experts were sent to the war-devastated country to conduct a general survey. So successful were their efforts that Poland asked for a similar "mission" of experts, and in 1947 a survey of agriculture in Poland was carried on by authorities from different countries, under the direction of FAO.

Then Siam called for help and later Venezuela—all within the first two years while Sir John was still director.

These "missions" were not expensive. Yet they brought to these countries some of the best experts of the world. They traveled extensively. They conferred with local authorities and obtained information from them. Then, when they were clear as to the best ways of improving agriculture in that nation, they submitted a report to it and to the FAO. The mission had no power to act, but it could advise. Here was an inexpensive way of sharing expert knowledge from all over the world and putting it to work for the improvement of conditions in a single country. As a result of such missions the entire world would eventually be affected.

Still another way of sharing the expert knowledge of the world was to call international conferences where top-notch scientists could exchange information and ideas. Here was a real service FAO could perform, and again with little expense.

So FAO brought together in India a group of experts on raising rice in Asia. Pooling their knowledge led to the increased and more efficient raising of this staple for nearly one half of the world's peoples.

Insects are one of the most deadly enemies of crops. They destroy food in the field and food when it is stored. FAO wanted to save every bit of food that it could. So it called together in London in 1947 leading experts from twenty-seven nations and enabled them to share their knowledge on insect control.

Similar conferences were held in these early months on timber production in Europe and on the increase of cereals for export from forty nations whose representatives met in Paris.

Out in the Near and Middle East one of the chief problems is securing an adequate water supply. At the request of the governments in that part of the world, FAO sent a team of experts to help them with better ways of drilling deep wells and establishing adequate irrigation systems.

Peru was faced with the problem of modern refrigeration and storage facilities to preserve its food supply. They called for help and the FAO responded by sending a team of authorities to that small South American country.

More dramatic than any of these missions was the campaign against rinderpest in China and other Asiatic countries. Rinderpest is the most deadly disease among cattle in that part of the world. When it strikes a herd, nine out of ten animals are likely to die. As a result there is less food, and famine is likely to follow. In China rinderpest kills a million head of cattle yearly. A new vaccine had been developed by Canadian and American scientists during the war, and so a laboratory was set up in China and an extensive campaign begun to eradicate rinderpest from entire provinces of China. Similar campaigns were undertaken in other Asiatic countries.

The United States profited, too, from this international exchange of ideas in agriculture. The University of New Hampshire wanted disease-resistant bell peppers, and FAO experts found such improved products in Kansu Province in China. The Oklahoma Agricultural and Mechanical College was looking for muskmelons which could be raised in a dry climate, and FAO found such melons in another part of China. The University of California wanted apricots which were not susceptible to late spring frosts, and these were also found in China and Siam.

Hundreds of such examples could be cited of the exchange of information, with FAO acting as a clearinghouse for the world.

Still another method which they started to use in these early months was that of demonstration schools. Three such schools were set up in 1947 to enable Europeans to catch up with new methods which they had not known about because of the war. One of these was to demonstrate the use of hybrid corn. Another was to show them methods of artificial insemination for increasing their supply of cattle. A third was to illustrate the latest veterinary techniques developed in various countries.

Food from the sea was another concern of FAO. Since so few people in the Orient can expect to obtain meat, fish is their best bet for adding protein to their diet. So the FAO established an Indo-Pacific Fisheries Council to help those countries develop their fisheries.

This list might be continued, for FAO did much in those early months to carry out its motto, "*Fiat panis* [Let there be bread]."

Sir John had accepted the director generalship of FAO for a two year term, and at the end of that time he resigned. He had gotten the organization off to a good start. Now he could retire to his farm in Scotland and concentrate on some of the other concerns he had for building a better world.

He could leave now with a feeling of accomplishment. As he said on the occasion of his retirement, "I warned the FAO Conference in Quebec that it would be a miracle if FAO ever succeeded, but that as we live in an age of miracles we must try, because there was no other hope for humanity. If FAO failed, the world would drift into chaos. . . . The miracle is taking place! If FAO had done nothing else but warn governments and get the International Emergency Food Council started, it was well worth all the money that has been spent on it. But other things have been done. . . . More timber is coming into Europe today than would have come if it were not for the action taken by FAO. . . . There are plans for the Middle East, which, if approved, will lead to increased food production on many thousands of acres in 1949. We have a hundred technicians in underdeveloped and war-devastated countries, sent at the request of governments to help them to produce more food. . . ."

Then, as if in summary of a lifetime dream, he closed by saying, "It is difficult to get nations to co-operate on a political level. The world is torn by political strife. But through FAO the nations are co-operating. Here round the Council table representatives of governments are not talking about war, not thinking about war. They are planning for the greatest movement that will make for peace—increased food production, the strengthening of agriculture, and food for the people of the world."

He had accomplished much and the world knew it. In England he was made a baron and from now on he would be known as Lord Boyd Orr. And in Norway the Parliament awarded him the Nobel Prize for Peace, the highest honor of this kind which can be awarded anyone.

When Orr gave the customary speech in Oslo in accepting this world peace award, he outlined his basic philosophy about the changing world in which we live. It was a powerful speech —one of the best he had ever given, and he had made many brilliant speeches.

"We have reached the end of the age of competing empires," he said. "Science has produced such powerful weapons that in a war between great powers there would be neither victor nor vanquished. Both would be overwhelmed in destruction. Our civilization is now in the transition stage between the age of warring empires and a new age of world unity and peace."

After tracing the development of modern science and its impact on our modern world, he continued, "The thunderbolt of Jove was a pipsqueak compared to the atomic bomb, Mercury, the messenger of the Gods with wings on his heels, a slow coach compared with radio, and the magic carpet of the fairy tale a crude method of travel compared with a transatlantic liner." The trouble with the world today, he said, was the "difficulty of adjusting human society to this terrific impact of modern science."

Looking ahead, as he had done all his life, he foresaw either world suicide or a world society governed by a world government. "We are now moving from conquest to union by consent, each state with a government controlling its own internal affairs, but united by a central government with laws to regulate interstate affairs and put an end to war within the Union." Then, in one of his famous punch lines, he asserted, "The only alternative to war is the United States of the World."

He then looked back for a moment to various attempts at establishing such a world government. Concerning the League of Nations he said, "The great conception of the League was premature because politicians, highly skilled in the old diplomacy of foreign affairs, did not realize that nineteenth century politics and economics will not carry twentieth century science.

They reconstituted the postwar shattered world on the old model. It wobbled in the 1929 economic crisis and crashed in a second world war."

Of the new United Nations he had this to say, "The UN is a better organization than the League." And the reason?—the specialized agencies—which are "the machinery through which governments can join in eliminating hunger, poverty, and disease, and in creating prosperity in agriculture, industry, and trade which will be permanent because based on the needs of the people which do not fluctuate in booms and slumps."

He expressed his disappointment, however, over the support given to these agencies of the UN. "If the sixty governments which adhere to these and have given the great ideal of cooperation lip service would agree to devote to them one unit of their currency for every hundred they are devoting to preparation for war, and allow them freedom of action, I venture to predict that within a few years the political issues which divide nations would become meaningless and the obstacles to peace disappear."

Orr sensed the need for some nation, preferably one of the most powerful ones, to take the lead in a positive program for peace. On this theme he said, "The nation or group of nations which will make a great new gesture of friendship and an offer to collaborate with all governments in a simple and concrete world plan of development would win the allegiance of the people of all countries, who are sick to death of political conflict and preparation for war. The government which is strongest and surest of itself is the one which should take the lead in this road to peace."

Next he turned to the role of individuals in creating world community. "In the last resort," he maintained, "the decision of peace or war lies with the people. Even in totalitarian countries the leader must now justify his actions in the eyes of the people. . . . If the peoples of the world get together and with one united voice demand world unity and peace, they will get it. It is the duty of every person of intelligence and good will to support one or another of the international people's organizations."

He concluded by predicting that peace was inevitable for European civilization. "It can be either the peace of the grave —or a new dynamic peace applying science in a great leap forward in the evolution of human society to a new age in which hunger, poverty, and preventable diseases will be eliminated from the earth—an age in which the people in every country will rise to a far higher level of intellectual and cultural well-being, an age in which 'iron curtains' will disappear and people, though intensely patriotic for their own country, will be able to travel freely as world citizens."

When one reads this moving speech, he should not be surprised to know that Lord Boyd Orr gave part of the Nobel Peace Prize money for the building of a Peace Center in London where the National Peace Council and other similar organizations could have offices and continue their work more effectively. Nor should one be surprised to know that Lord Boyd Orr has become president of the World Movement for a World Government.

In the years since the Nobel Peace Prize was awarded to him he has been most active in the various movements to increase world understanding and establish a world government.

This is the great passion of his life, to which he is devoting all his energies nowadays.

Someday a statue of him will be placed in a World Hall of Fame as a great hunger fighter, a great statesman, a great supporter of world government, a great citizen of the world.

ELEANOR ROOSEVELT

Defender of Human Rights

It was evening on one of those scorching hot days in which India specializes. But the heat meant little to a thousand Indians who waited outside the Taj Mahal Hotel, for they had heard that Eleanor Roosevelt was in Bombay and they would endure almost anything to see her. Patiently and excitedly they waited for her to appear.

On the dot she sped out of the front door and headed for the waiting automobile. Shouts and applause accompanied her every step of the way.

Then, instead of sitting down in the car, she stood, bowed her head and folded her arms in the Hindu posture of *namaskar*.

The crowd burst forth with "Eleanor Roosevelt *zindabad!* Eleanor Roosevelt *zindabad* [Long live Eleanor Roosevelt]!"

She dropped her hands and started to sit down, but they continued their chant. Again and again she made this gesture of friendship while the crowd roared.

At last the car started to move and the crowd watched and waved and shouted until it disappeared down the street.

This was merely one incident in another triumphant tour to a far corner of the earth. But it was characteristic of Mrs. Roosevelt. She had learned how people greeted each other in this country and she had adapted herself to their ways. In a gracious and simple gesture she had told them that they were friends. They sensed her sincerity and her friendliness and responded enthusiastically.

To them and to millions like them all over the globe she was the widow of the great Franklin Delano Roosevelt. But she was much more than that. She was a person in her own right—the First Lady of the United Nations and the First Lady of the World. She was the champion of the underprivileged, the friend of the forgotten, the defender of human rights for everyone, everywhere. Above all she was a person who was sensitive to others, warm, and full of human understanding.

She had taken this particular trip in 1952 to inform herself on conditions in the Near and Middle East and in Southeast

Asia. Her duties as a United States delegate to the United Nations General Assemblies and as a member of the UN Commission on Human Rights demanded that she have fresh, first-hand information, and she was out to get such material. As she said upon her arrival in New Delhi, "I have come to learn."

Later she would write a book about her impressions which would help to inform other people about the countries which she had seen.

Unofficially she was representing the United States and the United Nations as she moved from Beirut to Damascus, on to Amman, Jerusalem, and Tel Aviv, through Karachi to New Delhi, Bombay, and Calcutta, over to Bangkok, Singapore, and Manila, and thence back to San Francisco and Hyde Park. Unofficially, too, she was building the defenses of democracy in the minds and hearts of men and women in one of the most densely populated and strategic parts of the world. She was an ambassador-at-large—without portfolio.

On this globe-encircling journey she did what she had done so many times before when she had visited almost every other part of the world. She inspected hospitals, clinics, and child centers. She visited factories, irrigation projects, and experimental farms. She took a look at schools, research centers, and slums.

Those were the places she wanted to see. Then, in deference to the wishes of her hosts and hostesses, she spoke at banquets and public meetings, received honorary degrees from colleges and universities, made broadcasts over local and national radios, and attended receptions of every kind.

At such meetings she was feted and honored and praised. The Vice-Chancellor of the Aligarh University in India introduced her as "the most popular living American and the most admired woman of the world today." Vice-President Benegal Rau, who had worked with her in the UN, referred to her as an American phenomenon comparable to Niagara Falls. Prime Minister Nehru called her "one of the greatest personalities of the day, . . . a great woman, . . . a representative of a resurgent humanity."

Such praise was truly deserved. But to those who knew her life story it all seemed strange. Such a place in the sun would not have been predicted for her by anyone who had known her as a child. Certainly none of her relatives or friends would have guessed that she would someday become the most admired and the most influential woman in the world.

And why not? Because as a girl she was a plain, shy child whom few praised. Little had they guessed that her life would be a long and continuous struggle to overcome her shyness, to compensate for her appearance, and to win the respect and affection of others. Nor had they guessed how successful she would be on all three counts.

Her life began in New York City on October 11, 1884, in a big mansion on West Thirty-seventh Street. The family had money and belonged to society. Eleanor's mother was "one of the most beautiful women" she had ever seen. But she lacked the ability to understand her daughter and sometimes made life very difficult for her. She nicknamed Eleanor "Granny" and explained to visitors that the name was given to her because she was "such a funny child, so old-fashioned." She made Eleanor learn Bible verses and recite them to her every morning.

Writing about her mother years later, Eleanor said that "she had such high standards of morals that it encouraged me to wrongdoing. I felt that it was utterly impossible for me ever to live up to her."

Her most pleasant memories of her mother are of the evenings when she was dressing for some social function. Eleanor would stand and watch her dress and admire her beauty from a distance. And when her mother had one of her frequent headaches, Eleanor would sometimes stroke her head. Then she would feel useful and loved.

The only real affection that she got was from her father. She adored him and wanted to be with him as much as possible. But Elliott Roosevelt had become an alcoholic and spent most of his time in various sanatoria, always hoping that he would be cured.

She looked forward to his infrequent visits, since he was the center of her life. When he did return, they would go riding together or she would dance for him and his friends. Instead of being called "Granny," she was then called "Nell," and she loved her father for that affectionate name. As she records it, "He dominated my life as long as he lived and was the love of my life for many years after he died."

Her traveling began early, for when she was five and a half the whole family went to Paris. Eleanor was a bit of a nuisance to have around, so she was placed in a convent. There she learned French in order to play with the other girls, but she was a foreigner and a Protestant and not particularly welcome as a playmate. It was not a good experience for a lonely little girl who longed for affection and praise.

When she was eight her mother died and two years later her father also passed away. At ten she was mighty miserable and her grandmother, with whom she was sent to live, didn't help her much.

Grandmother Hall had been brought up in a strait-laced society with the strings pulled *tight*, and she expected everyone else to be brought up in the same way.

Eleanor was dressed from November to April in flannels from her neck to her ankles. She was growing rapidly, but the dresses that were made or picked out for her were often above her knees, even though all the other girls wore dresses halfway down their legs. High-buttoned shoes were the fashion, but on a skinny, long-legged girl they only emphasized her height.

The Halls were highly educated people, but it was not the kind of education that Eleanor found particularly useful. She had to spend long hours at the piano, even though she had no interest or talent in music. She had to memorize verse after verse from the Bible *in French*, but wasn't taught to think or reason. She could attend the plays of Shakespeare, but none of the popular plays of her day.

And to build her up physically cold sponge baths were prescribed for her every morning.

It was hardly the kind of life that one would look back on with pleasure!

Eleanor did what many other children would do in the circumstances: she escaped into a dream world of her own, with her father as the hero and herself as the heroine. In the summers when she went to the country with her grandmother, often she took refuge in her own room on rainy days and read. In her *Autobiography* she tells about reading a book called *Misunderstood*, of crying bitterly, and having "a good time."

There were really good times, however, even in this strict

and adult circle. Her Aunts Pussie and Maude and her Uncles Vallie and Eddie played games with her, took her riding, and sometimes took her on camping trips. And the washerwoman let her wash and iron and occasionally took her to her own house to spend a day.

She had a dog and a pony to love, and they were a great joy to her. She liked her ballet lessons, too.

Things took a turn for the better in the autumn of 1899 when she was sent to school near London. The girls in Allenswood were required to talk all day in French, but that was easy for Eleanor. She had learned French before she had learned English—from a French governess—and she had learned more in the convent in France. The head of the school, a Mademoiselle Souvestre, liked Americans and had had Eleanor's aunt as a pupil years before. That helped a shy young girl from the States to feel at home almost from the beginning.

Mlle. Souvestre was an attractive person, had traveled widely, had friends in many countries, and was keenly interested in current world affairs. She expected the girls in her school to work hard and set high standards for them in scholarship.

All this challenged Eleanor and she responded well. Soon she was chosen to sit opposite the headmistress at meals and to go with her on trips during vacation periods. She spent many hours in her room with this gifted teacher, listening to her read poems, plays, and stories in French. And she wrote papers for her on current topics as a part of a class for special students picked out by the headmistress.

Mlle. Souvestre was also a champion of lost causes. Those were the days of the famous Dreyfus case in France, and Mlle. Souvestre was one of those who defended his innocence for years until he was finally judged not guilty by the courts. Most of the girls were pro-English during the Boer War in Africa, but Mlle. Souvestre was pro-Boer. She believed in freedom of thought and would declare a holiday for English victories in that conflict, but she would shut herself in her room or spend the day with the non-English girls on such holidays.

This remarkable woman helped to fill the place in Eleanor's life which her father's death had left. Years later when Mrs. Roosevelt was asked by *Look* magazine to name the seven persons who had influenced her most during her life, she listed Mlle. Souvestre as one of the seven. Writing about her, she said, "She exerted perhaps the greatest influence on my girlhood. . . . For three years I basked in her generous presence, and I think those three years did much to form my character and give me confidence to go through some of the trials that awaited me when I returned to the United States."

Eleanor was now eighteen. She had traveled all over Europe. She had had a good education in the best tradition of those days. Grandmother Hall thought it was time that she came home. A girl of eighteen should be introduced to society and begin to think of marriage to the "right man," which meant a socially acceptable person.

So Eleanor came back to New York City and was properly introduced into the society to which the Halls and the Roosevelts had belonged for many generations.

She went to all the right parties, met all the right people, and did all the right things. But she didn't do them very well. She had lived largely with older people and girls and felt shy and ill at ease with most of the boys. She didn't dance well and was gangly and awkward on the dance floor.

So the next season she rebelled against much of the routine of social life in the younger set. She spent most of her time in what she thought were more constructive activities. She taught at the Rivington Street Settlement House and helped the women of the Consumers' League. Much of her time was devoted to her younger brother Hall.

It looked as if Eleanor would be a useful citizen but that she would become an old maid. Franklin Roosevelt thought differently. He had met his fifth cousin at family parties and found her intelligent and charming. She had traveled widely and read a lot and was not just another silly girl caught in the social whirl. She wasn't particularly pretty but she did have beautiful hair, attractive eyes, and interesting hands. Besides, beauty was only skin-deep!

So he courted her for a short time and then asked her to marry him. She was then nineteen and he was twenty-one. Their families were a little surprised, but pleased. Just to make sure that they were in love, Franklin was sent on a cruise in the West Indies and Eleanor remained with an aunt in New York City.

One can just imagine how the tongues wagged that winter. The "ugly duckling" had made the best catch of the season. Franklin Roosevelt was handsome, wealthy, belonged to one of the best families, and was a graduate of Groton and Harvard. He was suave and debonair. What more could anyone want? And Eleanor was his choice!

The wedding was held in New York City on St. Patrick's Day, March 17, 1905. "Uncle Ted" Roosevelt, the President of the United States, was to be in town for the big parade that day and he could stay on in the city to give the bride away. It was also the birthday of Eleanor's mother, which gave it added significance.

Eleanor did not know much about housekeeping, but her mother-in-law supervised just about everything. Franklin was still a student at the Columbia University Law School, and so the honeymoon was postponed until the following summer, when they went to Europe and saw Paris, Milan, Venice, Rome, London, Edinburgh, and all the other favorite spots of tourists.

According to Eleanor Roosevelt the next ten years were spent in raising babies. In 1906 Anna was born, in 1907 James, and in 1910 Elliott. A third child, named Franklin, Jr., died in infancy, but in 1914 another boy was born and he was given the same name. In 1916 John came into the family. Meanwhile Eleanor was continuing to look after her younger brother Hall, who was like an older brother to her growing family. The winters were spent in New York City and the summers in the family place in Canada.

There were servants to help Mrs. Roosevelt, so she had some time on her hands. She brushed up on her French, Italian, and German, and read almost every "best seller" which appeared.

Franklin worked for a time in a law firm in New York City. But he was eager to enter politics, partly due to the influence of Teddy Roosevelt, who was urging young men to forget that public service was supposed to be "dirty" and to go into it and help clean it up.

Franklin was a Democrat and almost everyone else in his district was a Republican. The only way he could win was to get acquainted with people personally. So he set out to visit every store and village and town and to win friends. He worked hard and won. He was the first Democratic state senator from that district in thirty-two years!

This was the first rung on the political ladder by which Franklin Roosevelt rose to the presidency of the United States. The rungs in between were an assistant secretaryship of navy in 1913 under Woodrow Wilson, his candidacy for Vice-President in 1920 (in which he was defeated), and his election to the governorship of New York in 1928 and again in 1930.

This meant all kinds of adjustments to Mrs. Roosevelt. She knew very little about politics. In fact she knew so little that she had been unable on their honeymoon abroad to explain the difference between the state and federal governments in the United States.

But she has always been a determined woman. It was her duty to learn, and she learned slowly but exceedingly well.

In Albany she began to lead the dual life which she was destined to follow for most of her life. Part of her life was to be private. Increasingly the other part was to be devoted to public affairs.

Her education in politics began in her own home. In the State Senate Franklin soon became the leader of a group of young liberals. They met in his house before sessions at the capitol, and many times in the evening. Eleanor's job was to manage the household and see that the guests were comfortable. Her second task was to be able to get along with all kinds of people. As she tells it, "Anyone who came was grist to my mill, because I was beginning to get interested in human beings, and I found that almost everyone had something interesting to contribute to my education."

A trip to New Mexico opened up other vistas for her. She had known Europe, but not the United States. Now she was beginning to know her own country. "Instead of reading about it in a book, I was seeing it—and I was thrilled."

When Franklin became Assistant Secretary of the Navy, he was obliged to make numerous trips and on many of them Eleanor accompanied him. They were strenuous trips, too, but she began to realize she had an unusual amount of endurance. This further strengthened her confidence in herself.

World War I meant a changed existence for Mrs. Roosevelt. There was considerable entertaining to do at home for the friends of her husband who were in the United States on missions. There was work in the Red Cross canteens for the soldiers. There was her own large family to care for. And there was knitting and sewing at all possible odd moments.

She met all kinds of people and gradually learned that "practically no one in the world is entirely bad or entirely good." As she puts it, "I had spent most of my life in an atmosphere where everyone was sure of what was right and what was wrong, and as life has progressed I have gradually come to believe that human beings who try to judge other human beings are undertaking a somewhat difficult job." Her advice? "When your duty does not thrust ultimate judgments upon you, perhaps it is as well to keep an open and charitable mind, and to try to understand why people do things instead of condemning the acts themselves."

During this period she visited in hospitals a great deal and came to know the conditions in those places intimately. She was most horrified by the crowded conditions and lack of care in the section of St. Elizabeth's Hospital in Washington where the shell-shocked patients were kept. She felt that something needed to be done and so she contacted the Secretary of the Interior, Franklin K. Lane. Eventually an investigation was carried on and Congress increased the appropriation for this mental hospital. Her initiative in this instance undoubtedly hastened the day when St. Elizabeth's would be one of the best institutions in the United States for the care of mentally disturbed patients.

In 1920 Franklin Roosevelt had been nominated for Vice-President on the Democratic ticket, with James Cox of Ohio. Against them were pitted Warren G. Harding and Calvin Coolidge. It was on the campaign trips that year that Eleanor became well acquainted with Louis Howe, who was to mean so much to her husband and to her in the years ahead, as Franklin's secretary, closest friend, and adviser, and as her teacher. Through him she came to respect the newspapermen who went with them everywhere.

Cox and Roosevelt were badly defeated and Franklin returned to New York City to the practice of law. It looked as if life would be more leisurely for Eleanor now. So she took cooking lessons and shorthand and typewriting lessons. The League of Women Voters asked her to keep track of national legislation in Washington and write reports for their members. She accepted appointment to the boards of various charities.

But Fate had other plans in store for both the Roosevelts. During the summer of 1921 Franklin had a serious stroke of infantile paralysis and it looked for a time as if he might be an invalid for the rest of his life. His mother decided that he should retire to Hyde Park and live out the remainder of his years in a wheel chair or in bed.

Eleanor thought differently. "He is not an invalid," she said. "A renewed interest in life is what he needs. Association with his friends and as much activity as he can stand, as his strength comes back, will be the best thing in the world for him."

This was a declaration of independence from her mother-in-law. The doctor sided with Eleanor. The result was one of the most remarkable stories of human rehabilitation in history.

Louis Howe gave up his plans for a business of his own and came to live with the Roosevelts and to advise and counsel Eleanor. He urged her to entertain as much as possible so that Franklin could keep in touch with politics and politicians. And he urged her to become as active as possible in all kinds of political activities. In that way she would keep busy, establish and maintain Franklin's contact with politics, and keep him interested in something outside himself and his illness.

During the course of the next few years she led a strenuous but interesting life. She began to raise funds for the women's division of the New York State Democratic Committee. She presided at luncheons. She edited a news sheet for the party. She spoke here and there, gradually becoming a good speaker, even though her nervousness never completely disappeared.

Meanwhile she was busy with the children. They adored Franklin and seldom thought of him as an invalid, but there were many things he could not do with them. Eleanor had had some unfortunate experiences in the water as a child, but she overcame her fear and learned to swim. The same was true with horseback riding. She had never done much camping, but small boys needed this experience, so she went on camping trips with them. She was now a quite different person from

168

the shy, fearful little girl described in the earlier part of this chapter. In her *Autobiography* she refers to these years as the period of her "intensive education."

She had had the courage to gamble with fate, and by 1928 her faith and her tenacity had won. Franklin had recovered enough by then to run for governor of New York State. That was the year that Al Smith was the Democratic candidate for President. Smith lost, but Roosevelt won. In 1928 and again in 1930 he was elected governor of the largest state in the United States, despite the fact that he was a cripple and could move about only with great difficulty.

Eleanor did a great deal as the wife of the Governor, but her greatest contribution was probably her service as "eyes and feet" for her husband. Wherever they went she did the walking about, the careful inspection into hospitals, homes for the aged and infirm, prisons, schools, and other institutions. Her reports had to be very accurate, for Franklin demanded the most minute details.

But he had trained her well for such work. She has described her training in the art of observation in this fashion: "Just sitting with him in the observation car at the end of a train, I learned how to watch the tracks and see their condition, how to look at the countryside and note whether there was soil erosion and what condition the forests and fields were in. As we went through the outskirts of a town or village I soon learned to look at the clothes on the wash line and at the cars and to notice whether houses needed painting. . . . My husband opened the windows of the world for me. As I think it over, he was perhaps the greatest teacher of the many who contributed to my education."

In 1932 this "team" moved into the White House as President and First Lady of the United States.

Life there would not be easy, but it would call upon every bit of Eleanor's ability. Fortunately she brought to this task "a Spartan character, the curiosity of a house detective, and the energy of a mountain goat," as one reporter described her.

Almost every President's wife had kept pretty much out of the limelight. They had entertained, shaken hands at receptions, acted as honorary chairmen of various organizations, and been photographed. But Eleanor was different. She had developed a personality of her own and she did not intend to become a nonentity. Besides, the President needed her help badly.

So during the first seven years in the White House she delivered hundreds of lectures, wrote a million words, traveled nearly three hundred thousand miles, and shook half a million hands.

It was difficult for Franklin to travel, but he could rely on his wife to crisscross the nation to visit hospitals, inspect housing projects, dedicate public health centers, and report on the condition of the coal miners.

Those early years in the White House were depression years and, as the President pointed out so eloquently, one third of the nation was "ill-housed, ill-fed, ill-clothed." He was deeply concerned with such conditions. Part of this concern was his own; part of it was a reflection of Eleanor's championship of the underprivileged.

For years she had been studying and helping the forgotten men and women. She saw no reason why she should stop just because she was the President's wife. If anything, she increased her efforts on their behalf. She championed the cause of equal rights for Negroes. She supported the establishment of the Civilian Conservation Corps and the National Youth Administration to help the young people caught in the depression. She sought better conditions for sharecroppers, slum dwellers, and tenant farmers. She allied herself with the labor movement and backed their demands for collective bargaining. She played an active role in the improvement of child welfare and maternal care. She was the champion of the "general welfare" clause of the Constitution.

People criticized her unmercifully, relentlessly. They called her a busybody, a snoop, a radical, and many uprintable names. She ignored their insults and went about doing good, aiding people in need wherever she found them.

Her radio work and her writing brought in a sizable income, but she turned the proceeds over to various charities and organizations in which she was interested.

People criticized her husband, too. Sometimes they did this in front of her. One instance of such open criticism occurred after a public speech when a woman rose in the audience and asked, "Isn't it true, Mrs. Roosevelt, that the President's illness affected his mind?" Eleanor paused a moment and responded quietly, "Yes, I think it did. I think it made him more sensitive to the feelings of suffering people."

She was a busy person, for most of these activities had to be sandwiched in between official receptions and entertainment in the White House, which she carried on in a simple and gracious manner. But as one writer has said, "She had the superb quality of never being too busy to be kind."

When the United States entered World War II, she was

busier than ever. There was her husband to care for. There were innumerable visitors from abroad to entertain in addition to those from the United States. There was her work for a few months in the Office of Civilian Defense under the leadership of LaGuardia.

Her most important service, however, to Franklin and to the nation were the long and tiring trips abroad to see what was going on in different parts of the world. The first of these was to England in 1942. On this trip it was necessary for her to have a code name as a safety measure. Somehow she acquired the name "Rover." She never knew who coined it, but she always suspected her husband!

In England she worked from early in the morning till very late at night. She made tours into the camps where the servicemen were stationed, observed the work of the Women's Voluntary Services, interviewed government officials, and observed the ways in which civilian defense was carried on. All her keen observations were reported to the President and to the proper authorities in the States. Then, in her spare time, she wrote or phoned the families of many of the servicemen she had met.

The next trip was a short one with Franklin to Mexico to inspect some war plants and to increase the feeling of being good neighbors.

Then came a similar but even more dangerous journey to Australia, New Zealand, and seventeen islands in the Pacific. On that trip she lost thirty pounds and when she got home she realized she was "more tired than I had ever been in all my life."

In 1944 there was a third trip, this time to the Caribbean area and as far south as Brazil.

These war years with their staggering responsibilities had sapped the strength of the President and towards the end of the war the family and his close friends knew that he was not well. In April 1945 he went back to Warm Springs, Georgia, where he had spent so many months and from which he always returned in better spirits and in better health. News came to Washington that he was ill, but the secret service men asked Eleanor to continue her activities in the capital so as not to alarm the nation. Then he suffered a stroke and died on April 12 before she could reach him.

It was a blow to the nation, and to the world. It was a personal tragedy for Mrs. Roosevelt. She called Vice-President Truman and asked him to come to the White House. After she had told him the news, he turned to her and inquired, "What can I do for you, Mrs. Roosevelt?" And her reply was, "What can we do for you?" Yes, even at a time like that she was not too busy or too bereaved to think of others, to think of the kindly word—and to say it.

Within a few days she left the White House, after more than twelve years there. For many persons that would have meant the end of a public career. She was then sixty-one and could easily have retired.

But not Eleanor Roosevelt. There was work to be done in the world and if she could be useful she would do her part.

That fall President Truman appointed her as one of the United States delegates to the First General Assembly of the United Nations. This was the organization which her husband had planned so carefully and one which she had supported from the very first. It was an appropriate appointment.

She did not know too much about her job, but she soon

learned. When she accepted the appointment she said, "I hope I can deserve the confidence of those who appointed me and the good will and respect of those who work with me."

She soon accomplished both aims. Her colleague Senator Vandenberg, a leading Republican, was soon able to say, "She is doing a splendid job. She has made a fine impression on all the other delegations. I want to say that I take back everything I ever said about her—and believe me, it's been plenty."

In April 1946 she was elected chairman of the United Nations Commission on Human Rights. She began at once a careful study and analysis of all the problems connected with this job, for she had made it a lifelong rule to be well informed on any topic on which she was speaking and writing. Once the Charter was framed, she began work with her colleagues on the Covenant of Human Rights, which is intended to serve as a treaty which nations will sign and thereby bind themselves to support.

This work has been very close to her heart, for it carried out on a world scale the defense of human rights for which she had worked so hard in her state and then on a nationwide scale.

All this work was extremely important to the world. As Trygve Lie, the first Secretary General of the United Nations, has said, this Charter of Human Rights is "destined to become one of the great documents of history."

In a way this work with the United Nations became the climax of her life. To it she has given her time, her energy, and her remarkable ability.

All through these busy years she continued to keep in constant and intimate touch with her children and grandchildren, having them with her in the summer time, picking out Christmas gifts for them on her many trips, telephoning and writing them frequently.

Meanwhile the world has clamored to hear and see her. When a statue to President Roosevelt was to be unveiled in London, she was invited to participate in the ceremony. And she went. One of the large and influential London newspapers reporting on the event summarized her life by saying, "She has walked with kings, but never lost the common touch." There have been many such trips to every part of the United States and to many parts of the world.

Everywhere she has been acclaimed as one of the great women of this generation. Lebanon and El Salvador have placed her picture on their stamps. A forest in Palestine has been named after her. Universities in the United States, England, France, India have given her honorary degrees.

And the common people of many nations have honored her. In a recent poll of the leaders of a large women's magazine in the United States, she was voted the most popular living American of either sex. In 1948 the American Institute of Public Opinion took another poll and in it she was voted "the most admired woman living today in any part of the world."

Her lifetime struggle against shyness and loneliness has been successful. She has achieved the kind of maturity few people reach. She has become a citizen of the world.

DOMINGO SARMIENTO

Citizen of the New World

Every morning as Señora Laura strolled down the main street of San Juan, Argentina, she saw a sixteen-year-old dry goods clerk standing by the window reading a book. When she returned from morning mass, he would still be standing there. She would shake her head disapprovingly and mutter to herself, "There can't be anything good in that little fellow. If those were good books, he wouldn't read them so eagerly."

But Señora Laura was wrong. The "little fellow" who was always reading books after he had swept the store was Domingo Faustino Sarmiento. Someday he would be considered the greatest writer in Argentina. Later he would be ambassador to the United States and one of the champions of Pan-Americanism. Then he would be president of the Argentine Republic and one of its great reformers.

The book he was devouring when Señora Laura passed by was probably Franklin's *Autobiography*. Domingo read every book which he could find in his home town, but this one was his favorite. He read and reread it. He imagined that he was Franklin. Some day he too would become an honorary doctor and make his place in American letters.

And why would a book about Benjamin Franklin appeal so much to a shy young dry goods clerk in Argentina? Sarmiento

himself has written the answer in his own book, *Provincial Recollections*. In it he says, "No book has done me more good than his. . . . I felt that I was Franklin, and why not? Like him I was very poor and studious, and by scheming and following in his footsteps, I might one day form myself as he did. . . . His example is so stimulating and the career that he followed so within the reach of all, that no boy at all interested in self-improvement could fail to pattern himself on Franklin."

A little further in Sarmiento's account of his boyhood he speaks of Franklin's life again: "But young Franklin, though poor, destitute, and without any assistance but his own reason, labored with his hands to earn his living, superintended his own studies, and considered how he could improve his conduct and make his name famous, served his country by helping to rid it of its oppressors, and one day, having presented a simple device to the world to control the lightning from heaven, was able to boast of having saved millions of lives by his invention."

Some called Sarmiento's emulation of Franklin conceit. Others called it self-confidence and idealism. All through his life people who liked Sarmiento called him confident, assured, poised, certain. Those who disliked him called him conceited, egotistical, proud, contemptible. Yet it was this early belief in his own talent and his ability to succeed which helped Sarmiento to surmount seemingly insurmountable obstacles and to carry him through long periods of tumult and rebellion, both personal and national.

Domingo was born on February 15, 1811, in the city of San Juan, Argentina, almost in the shadow of the Andes. He was christened Faustin Valentin, but later he had his name changed to Domingo Faustino because of his mother's regard for the Dominican Order of monks.

His ancestors were members of two distinguished families— the Sarmientos and the Albarracines. His mother was an Albarracine and many members of that family had been writers, historians, teachers, philosophers, and religious leaders. They were also related to the Oro family, which was prominent in Argentinian affairs.

Domingo's immediate family, however, was poor and not at all prominent. They lived in a little mud-walled house surrounded by a yard with fig and orange trees, and beautiful, flaming flowers.

As a boy Domingo spent much of his time playing in the yard outside their tiny house. Near by his mother would sit at her spinning wheel placed in the shade of the fig tree. There she would weave the woolen cloth for friars' and monks' robes that earned her a few dollars to keep the family alive. Or sometimes she would make silk suspenders, scarfs, ties, and ponchos to send to Spain. She was an expert in weaving, knitting, and in making dyes. Like other women of her day she also baked, made candles, and made the clothes for Domingo and his four sisters.

Sometimes Domingo played alone and often he played with his sisters. When his mother was not looking he would some- times wander over to the pool and frighten the ducks to see what they would do. When the oranges in their three trees were ripe, he would help pick them, which was a special privilege.

Often he and his sisters would play war—like children all

over the world. Argentina and the other Spanish colonies had declared their independence from Spain, but a firm, stable government had not been set up. The Argentinians were mostly illiterate and not prepared for democratic government. As a result, various factions were struggling for control of the national government as well as for local control. There were frequent revolutions and the children would pretend that they were taking part in some of those fights.

Their interest in such warfare was whetted by the occasional visits of their father. He was a handsome, idealistic, but impractical man who never seemed able to settle down and support his family. Much of the time he was taking part in revolutions somewhere in Argentina. The children reveled in the stories of his exploits when he was at home and acted out what he had told them when he was away.

Sometimes Domingo would go with some of the older boys and men out onto the pampas or, on very special occasions, up the lower slopes of the Andes.

Occasionally the Sarmientos visited their rich relatives. But this was seldom, for Domingo's mother spurned their help. She preferred to be poor, uncomfortable, and independent rather than rich, comfortable, and dependent on them.

Domingo's father was determined that his boy should learn to read. He started him at the age of four on this road which Domingo was to travel all his life. Señor Sarmiento used to borrow learned works and insist that his son read every word from them. One of these was the *Critical History of Spain*, in four volumes. Most children would have been repulsed by such treatment, no matter how fine their father's intentions were but Domingo did not seem to resent this method of learning. In fact, he soaked up learning as a sponge soaks up water.

San Juan had established primary schools soon after independence had been declared and at the age of five Domingo was hustled off to one of these schools. Every day for nine years he attended, never missing a day. This was the best part of his early life. He liked school and devoured the few books that were available.

But he was not satisfied with the meager education he received at school. He borrowed books and read the Bible, a *Life of Cicero, Natural Theology and Evidences of Christianity,* and *The True Idea of the Holy See.* He studied the history of Greece and of Rome. There was no particular plan to all this reading. He merely read all the things he could find.

His education, however, was not limited to books. The people around him played a large part in his informal education. From his father he learned about political conditions in Argentina and other parts of South America and in Spain. One of his uncles taught him Latin and a local French engineer instructed him in mathematics and engineering.

The principal of the school, Don Ignacio Rodriguez, also took a special interest in this bright and enterprising boy. Rodriguez was a pioneer in education and interested in the latest methods of teaching. He read English, which was unusual in this Spanish-speaking country. He was fond of Domingo, whom he called "a most troublesome and vociferous reader."

The determination to follow in the footsteps of Franklin and the conditions at home made Domingo different from other children. He suffered some because of his uniqueness.

The chief difference between him and other children was his dislike of games. He was not adept in them and thought them a waste of time. He did, however, enjoy drawing.

Having to help run the family at an early age made him more serious than other children, too. As he said, "From the tender age of fifteen, I have been the head of my family. Father, mother, brothers, servants—everyone was subordinated to me, and this dislocation of natural relations has exerted a fatal influence upon my character. I have never recognized any authority excepting my own."

For a time it looked as if he might become a priest, the most respected profession in the country. But when he went to the seminary to prepare for the priesthood, several of the teachers were gone and conditions were such that he did not remain.

At fifteen he took up teaching, instructing pupils older than himself. At sixteen he began to work in the village store, but his life work was obviously not there. On the side he wrote essays, started a literary society, and opened a school.

Then his troubles began, troubles which were to change his life abruptly. Rosas was the dictator of Argentina at the time and a despot. He killed or exiled those who disagreed with him, and ruled the country with an iron hand. His local henchman was a man named Juan Facundo Quiroga.

Sarmiento did not agree with their tactics and was determined not to assist them in their dictatorship. One day he was ordered to close his shop and mount guard. He refused, adding that he would not serve under those "with whom we are oppressed." Trouble was in store for him. He was whipped and put in prison. As he wrote later, "In the eighteenth year of my life, I entered a jail and came out with a political opinion."

Within two years he had turned in his key to the store and had fled across the Andes Mountains to Chile. For years, then he shuttled back and forth between Argentina and Chile, according to the changes in government in his native land. Most of the time was spent in Chile, however, for he was almost always opposed to those in power in his own country.

For a while he taught school in Santa Rosa de los Andes. Then he ran an eating house in Procuro. Next he became a clerk in Valparáiso. Later he worked in the Majordomo mine in Chanarcillo.

All this time he was trying to satisfy his intellectual hunger. One of his employers testified to this fact when he said, "I have an amusing madman working for me. He spends hours reading out loud under the trees. If anyone asks him why he is reading, he says he is studying 'to be government.'"

While working in the mines, he tried each day to read one of Sir Walter Scott's great novels. A little later he tried to translate one of these into Spanish so that others might enjoy the work of this great novelist and so that he could improve his English.

Languages were the keys that could open up the literature of other countries to him, so he set up for himself a rigorous study plan. At eighteen he learned French, at twenty-two English, at twenty-six Italian, and at thirty-one Portuguese. He read all these well, but spoke them with a decided accent.

By the time he was twenty-five he was convinced that his life work was to help educate the common people. "Educate the sovereign," he kept saying, and by "the sovereign" he meant, of course, the people.

His first distinct contribution to education began in 1839

when he was twenty-eight years old. It was then that he founded a school for girls in San Juan. This was a radical idea in Argentina in those days—as it was in many other parts of the world.

The same year, with the help of friends who believed as he did, he started a newspaper, *El Zonda*, to combat tyrannical ideas and promote a spirit of democracy in his native land. Soon he began to publish pamphlets in which he criticized the government for its highhanded methods with the people. These booklets were vividly written and were eagerly read by the men and women of Argentina. He was clapped into jail, but escaped and started off for Chile again. Before he crossed the border this time he wrote on a rock near by the phrase which he repeated many times during life, "Ideas cannot be killed."

Back in Chile, he plunged into journalism, founding *The National* in Santiago and writing editorials and occasional articles for *The Mercury* in Valparáiso. The vigor and clarity of his writing soon won him the post of editor of *The Mercury*.

In these writings he was most concerned with the topics of freedom of worship, civil marriages, peace, and education. Shortly thereafter the Minister of Education of Chile made Sarmiento editor of *The National*. This was a great battleground for a great fighter and a profound thinker. Of his writing Sarmiento often said that he wrote like a fighter, "but my two fists are full of truths."

He was also interested in literature and the art of writing. In a famous newspaper battle with a well-known grammarian, Sarmiento stressed the danger of falling into barrenness and pedantry by following too closely the existing literary rules.

"It is the perversity of what one studies, the influence of grammarians, the respect towards admirable models, the fear of breaking rules, which has throttled the imagination of Chilean writers, which has turned into waste their generous nature and their capacity for genius. There is no spontaneity," he wrote. "There is only a jail whose door is guarded by the inflexible culture-ism. It beats down the unfortunate one who doesn't present himself with everything etiquette demands."

This was his criticism of the existing writing of his day. His alternative was: "Instead of occupying yourselves with form or gracefulness of style or with what Cervantes or Fray Luis Ponce de Leon once said, acquire new ideas wherever they come from, nourish your spirit with the manifestations of thought of the great figures of our epoch. Observe your country, the people, the customs, the institutions, the needs of today. Then write with love, from your heart, whatever you wish, whatever you can. That will be good basically, although the form may be incorrect. It will be passionate though at times not exact. The reader will like it although Garcilaso may rage. It will have no similarity with any other writing, but, good or bad, it will be your own."

All through these years he had been mulling over the most effective methods of educating the poor, illiterate masses of his own and other nations. He was convinced that progress would never come until the people were educated. The years were slipping by and he must act, but only in the most efficient manner. One dared not waste those precious possessions of time and energy. How could he best achieve his purpose?

The answer, he believed, was to start a training school for teachers in Santiago. By influencing a few of them, he could indirectly influence large numbers of people. So in 1842 he founded the first teacher education institution in South America, a landmark in the cultural development of that continent.

The next year he joined the faculty of the University of Chile and started to work on a school reader, which was published two years later and used by several generations of school children.

Then *Facundo—Civilization and Barbarism* appeared. It came out first in daily installments in the newspaper *Progress*. Soon it was on the presses as a book, a book much read and much discussed. It was called "the best known work in Argentina's literature" and "perhaps the most representative volume ever produced in the southern continent."

It was a great novel, a literary event. Yet it was more than that. It was a partially concealed bombshell. When one opened the covers, it did not burst. But as one read on, it (or the reader) grew warmer and warmer until the explosion came. What was the inflammatory substance which Sarmiento had scattered over the pages as he penned the book?

The first section deals with the life of a cowboy on the plains of Argentina and portrays the pride of the rancher in his supposed superiority over the city man. The second section describes Juan Facundo Quiroga, the chieftain of the San Juan region where Sarmiento had lived. In him were embodied the worst traits of the oppressor, forcing his subjects back into the barbarism from which they were beginning to emerge. Education is neglected. Christianity reverts to superstition. Civilization yields to barbarism. Here was feudal society at its worst. Here was the struggle between country and city. Here was the Argentina in which Sarmiento had lived.

And the remedies Sarmiento suggested? Education and immigration.

In the Argentine it was made a death penalty to publish or read anything which Sarmiento wrote. But people found ways to circumvent the law. They wanted to read what Sarmiento had written and he found ways of supplying them with the books. For instance, he wrapped a large crate of copies of *Facundo* with the ill-smelling asafetida and shipped the crate to a doctor friend marked, "Directions inside for its use against the whooping cough." The border authorities held their noses and quickly dispatched the crate to its destination.

Sarmiento was a troublesome character in the eyes of many, and his enemies were making matters mighty uncomfortable for him. Argentine officials brought pressure on the Chilean government to send him back to his own country where they could deal with him.

Fortunately the Chilean Minister of Education was a friend of Sarmiento. He did not intend to send him back to Argentina, but he had to do something to placate the Argentinian officials in order to keep peace between these two neighboring countries.

So Minister Montt asked Sarmiento to take a trip to Europe to study the educational systems there. Domingo agreed to this plan and spent the year 1845 in Uruguay and Brazil before setting off for Europe.

Once in Europe he visited France, Italy, Switzerland, Austria, Prussia, the Netherlands, and then France again. Everywhere he went during his two years abroad he observed schools, examined textbooks, and talked with teachers and specialists in various areas of education. He questioned them about their ideas of education and the methods and materials they were using.

He had expected to gain much from this continental tour, but he was disappointed until he reached England. There he chanced to pick up the *Seventh Annual Report* of Horace Mann, the Commissioner of Education for the state of Massachusetts. Sarmiento was intrigued with Mann's ideas on education and impressed with the progress of the new state-wide system of schools. Here was a man and a state government which was doing exactly what Sarmiento had dreamed of doing.

"After this important work fell into my hands," Sarmiento said, "I had a fixed point to which to direct myself." He hurried off to the United States and to West Newton, Massachusetts. He spent two memorable days with Horace Mann, a pioneer in public education and teacher training.

These two men had no common language which they could use easily, so Sarmiento spoke in French and Mrs. Mann translated the French into English for her husband. Then Horace Mann spoke in English and Mrs. Mann translated what he said into French for their visitor. It was a laborious way of communicating, but the only way in which they could exchange ideas.

This was a momentous experience and Sarmiento remained under the influence of it all his life. He became an ardent admirer of Horace Mann and attempted to adapt his ideas first in Chile and later in Argentina.

Horace Mann realized the stature of Sarmiento and his potential contribution to the educational systems of South

America. He arranged for him to meet Longfellow, Emerson, Channing, and other outstanding figures in the United States. He also arranged for him to lecture at the American Institute of Instruction and to receive an honorary degree from the University of Michigan.

Sarmiento traveled extensively in the United States and was deeply impressed with what he saw. He predicted a nation eventually of two hundred million with the Great Lakes area as the industrial center of the country. He was struck by the democratic atmosphere of the small towns and villages in the United States and amazed at the way in which North Americans traveled. In an account which he wrote of this trip in 1847 he said half-humorously, "If God were suddenly to call the world to judgment, He would surprise two thirds of the American population on the road like ants." He was impressed with the widespread system of roads and railroads and hoped that he could help to build such systems in Argentina someday. Above all he was affected by the concept of democracy and by the new idea of public education.

After a trip to the Middle West and a steamboat ride down the Mississippi, Sarmiento returned to Chile to give an account of his educational expedition. He collected his ideas on this trip abroad and published them in a volume entitled *Popular Education*. Later in the year he penned an account of the countries he had visited and printed them in a travel book, *Journeys Through Europe, Africa, and America*.

Sarmiento had had the feeling for a long time that the Spanish culture was in the decline. He felt that Argentina and the other South American countries would do well to establish closer cultural contacts with North America. This trip made him more certain of the wisdom of that course of action. From now on he would be even more outspoken as a champion of Pan-Americanism.

Some of his observations on the United States in his book, *Journeys Through Europe, Africa and America,* are overdrawn, but many of his remarks show keen powers of observation. One recent biographer has even gone so far as to say that "its insight into our American way of life and its description of the United States rival in places the works of de Tocqueville."

Shortly after his return to South America, Sarmiento married Doña Benita Martinez Pastoriza, a widow with a child of three. Sarmiento loved this child deeply and later wrote a book about him after he was killed while fighting in Paraguay.

Soon the opposition to Rosas in Argentina organized an attempt to overthrow the dictator and Sarmiento hastened to join these forces. In 1852 he took part in the battle at Monte Caseros, near Buenos Aires, which brought about the overthrow of this despot.

Within a few days Sarmiento saw that Rosas's successor would not bring too great a change from the dictatorial methods of his predecessor, and he went back again to Chile. There he edited *The Journal for Primary Schools,* a magazine for the Chilean ministry of education.

By 1855 Argentinian politics were calmer and Sarmiento moved to Buenos Aires to edit *The National.* This was an important job, but there was more important work for which there was no one so well qualified as he. Had he not founded the first teacher education institution in South America? Had he not become an authority on the educational systems of the United States and several European countries? Why should he not be used to help improve the educational system of his own country?

In 1856 he became director of the schools of Buenos Aires and from 1860 until 1864 Minister of Public Instruction of Argentina. This ministry had been established for the first time in 1859 while he was a state senator from Buenos Aires and he had taken an active part in setting it up.

In these two positions and later as President of the Argentine Republic, he conducted a crusade for more and better education. He was responsible for setting up hundreds of elementary schools throughout the nation and a few high schools and teacher training institutions. To improve agriculture he founded agricultural and veterinary schools and experimental farms. To assist the nation in exploiting its natural resources he created a School of Mines and introduced courses in engineering and science in the universities.

He also saw the need for educating the adults and started a system of traveling teachers to work with illiterates. The establishment of public libraries and museums was still another part of his vast program to bring education to Argentina.

Other countries in Latin America watched these developments with keen interest. Chile soon inaugurated a similar campaign, based on many of Sarmiento's ideas. Uruguay launched reforms which were destined to give it one of the best systems in the Western world. Costa Rica and Venezuela were also affected by the program inaugurated during this period in Argentina.

The climate of political opinion had now changed for the better in Argentina and a man of Sarmiento's manifold interests and abilities was in great demand. As a person with an interest in other countries and with linguistic ability, he was chosen first as Argentina's representative to Chile and Peru and then in 1865 as Minister Plenipotentiary and Envoy Extraordinary to the United States.

In recent years he had followed the career of Abraham Lincoln with tremendous respect. He had hoped to meet the Great Emancipator some day, but the assassination of Lincoln came before Sarmiento reached the United States.

After a brief visit with Mrs. Horace Mann, whose husband had died in 1859, Sarmiento settled in New York City, choosing that location because his work was to be more cultural and commercial than diplomatic.

Again he was impressed with the vitality, imagination, and growth in the United States. Most of all he was impressed with the western part of the nation and the strides it was making. He saw in its development a pattern for the expansion of Argentina. "Here," he wrote, "are attempted things that seem superhuman, inconceivable, absurd."

The importance of education was indelibly stamped upon his mind and he took voluminous notes for a future book, *The Schools, Basis of Prosperity in the Republic of the United States*. Upon his return to Argentina, he declared, "I have come from a country where education is everything, where education has succeeded in establishing true democracy, making races and classes equal."

He became grandiloquent at times in his praise of the States. In one such statement he declared that "South America is falling behind and will lose its God-given mission as part of modern civilization. Let us not hold up the United States in its forward march; that is what some are proposing to do. Let us overtake the United States. Let us be America, as the sea is the ocean. Let us be the United States."

Despite such lavish praise, he also saw some of the faults of the States. He warned against the rapid immigration which was being permitted without regard to selection or assimilation. He viewed with alarm the racial conflict being waged in those post-Civil War days, and warned that "against the violence and injustice of the Yankees there is no appeal on this earth."

While he was in the United States, his friends in Argentina were scheming to bring him home. In an election which is said to have been "the freest and most peaceful held in the republic," he was chosen President. He had not sought the office; the office had sought him.

On Columbus Day, October 12, 1868, he was inaugurated President of the land from which he had fled so many years ago and from which he had been in exile so much. The man who had long been studying "to be government" was now head of his nation.

His six years as President, from 1868 until 1874, were filled with trouble. There were Indian raids, uprisings in the provinces, floods, a drought which killed two million head of cattle, and a yellow fever epidemic in Buenos Aires which killed 13,500 people, or 8 per cent of the population, in 45 days.

But his administration helped push Argentina far ahead in political, economic, social, and educational affairs. During his term a railroad was built from Rosario to Córdoba. Plans were made for a national bank. A telegraph system was established. The school system which he had started as Minister of Public

Instruction was expanded and improved. From the United States he brought Benjamin Gould to build the first astronomical observatory in South America. With the help of Mrs. Mann he arranged for a large group of teachers from the United States to come to Argentina to help with the education there. He established a Committee on Popular Libraries.

Nor had he forgotten what he had learned in the United States about the importance of transportation and communication. During his administration railroad and telegraph lines were built to bind the country together and an ocean cable was laid to improve communication with other countries. Harbors were improved and mineral resources exploited.

His experiences as a journalist had impressed him with the power of the press in a democracy. He believed firmly in freedom of the press, even though he knew that there would be abuses of that freedom. "Let the press be governed by its instincts," he said. "By a single word it can save us from evils more lasting than the scratches it makes every day on the most illustrious reputations."

Argentina was a large country and sparsely populated. Sarmiento wanted more people and so he encouraged immigration. But he recalled his observations on unlimited immigration in the United States and so limited the number of people to be admitted each year.

Argentina had been allied with Brazil in a war against Uruguay. During his term as President, Sarmiento was able to conclude this disastrous conflict. He insisted that it should be ended without the addition of an inch of territory to Argentina. Historians agree that he "concluded as honorable peace with Paraguay as was ever negotiated."

He had had a vigorous and dynamic administration. Many men would have retired from active life after such a period of strenuous activity. But not Sarmiento. His life must count in the development of his country. The years remaining must be years of further accomplishment, he said.

A rapid review of the positions he held will give an idea of those next few years. In 1874 he was elected Senator from the Province of San Juan. In 1875 he became Director General of the schools in the Province of Buenos Aires. In 1877 he was appointed Minister of Interior. The year 1881 found him acting as General Superintendent of the Schools of Argentina and 1884 found him in Chile promoting the official translations of foreign books as an enrichment to that nation. Such translations, he felt, would do much to interpret the people of various countries to each other.

Meanwhile he was busy with his pen. When the national Congress of Argentina ordered the official publication of his complete works, there were fifty-two volumes. Only a few, however, were outstanding. *Facundo* heads the list. *The Life of Horace Mann* and *The Life of Abraham Lincoln* were good. His *Conflict and Harmony of Races in America*, referred to sometimes as *Facundo* grown old, is also widely read even today. His travelogues in book form were very popular. His educational reports contained much that is still applicable today.

Declining health finally caused him to move to Asunción, Paraguay, in 1887 for the milder climate it afforded. His daughter and granddaughter went with him to care for him in his declining days.

There, on September 11, 1888, he died.

His casket was wrapped in the flags of the four nations with which he had been most intimately associated. The flag of Argentina was one—the land where he had been born and of which he had become President. The flag of Chile was the second—the country in which he had spent so many years of his life and in which he had done so much of his journalistic and educational work. The flag of Paraguay was the third—for it was to Sarmiento that they were grateful for the just peace which terminated many years of hostility and war. And the flag of Uruguay was the fourth—because it was in that nation that his ideas had found their most receptive soil. The flag of the United States might well have been added, in view of his years there and his tremendous love and respect for her.

In reality, however, all nations may claim him as one of the great citizens of the world.

The tributes to him since his death have been many and varied. The great French sculptor Rodin was commissioned to carve a monument in marble to Sarmiento, which has been placed in Palermo Park in Buenos Aires.

On the hundredth anniversary of his birth Argentina printed a special stamp with the bust of Sarmiento on it and struck a medal in his honor, asserting that "Sarmiento was more than a citizen of Argentina, he was a citizen of the New World, called America."

At the international conference of Ministers and Directors of the American Republics held in Panama in 1943, they designated September 11 of each year as Teachers' Day, commemorating Sarmiento's death. In selecting Sarmiento as the man to honor by this special day, they referred to him particularly as "a teacher of teachers."

People have characterized Sarmiento and his contributions to the world in many different ways, yet all are agreed upon his greatness. A recent author, summarizing a century of Latin American thought, has said, "Sarmiento was the greatest of them all, the most thoroughly Argentine in spite of himself." Another writer has called him "the most powerful brain America has produced."

The Minister of Foreign Affairs of his home land said at the time of his death, "Argentine has lost one of its most eminent sons and America a noble apostle of liberty. Men like Sarmiento honor their country and are the glory of mankind."

ALBERT SCHWEITZER

Doctor in the Jungle

On Friday the thirteenth of October, 1905, a young man dropped a stack of letters into the letter box on Avenue de la Grande Armée in Strasbourg, Germany. On the outside they looked like ordinary letters. But the contents were far from ordinary.

When the parents and friends of the sender opened these innocent-looking messages, they were shocked. Albert Schweitzer, a brilliant and promising teacher, preacher, and musician, had decided to go to Africa as a medical missionary. He would soon give up his position as principal of the Theological College of St. Thomas and begin to study medicine to prepare himself for this new job in the jungles of Africa.

"Absurd," "ridiculous," "insane" were just a few of the adjectives his friends applied to his plan. Some people decided that he was going because he had been disappointed in love. Others said he was impatient over the growth of his professional plans. Most of them just couldn't understand. At the age of thirty he was the head of a famous school, one of the leading musicians in Europe, and a well-known minister. Why would he want to give up such a brilliant career to go to Africa?

One friend responded to Schweitzer's letter by writing, "Look here, old man, you're a general. Generals don't get themselves shot on the front line." Another told him he could earn enough money in Europe to support ten doctors or missionaries in Africa. Others pointed out that he was risking his life to go to that "dark continent" and his life was too valuable to lose.

Many were surprised by the suddenness of his decision. To Schweitzer it was not nearly so sudden. Years before he had resolved to go on enjoying his comparatively comfortable existence until he was thirty. From that time on he would devote himself to the "direct service of humanity."

Just what that particular service would be he had not known. For a time he thought he would work with abandoned or neglected children. He also considered work with tramps and discharged prisoners.

Then one evening he had picked up a magazine reporting on the activities of the Paris Missionary Society. As he thumbed through it, his eye caught the title of an article, "*Les Besoins de la Mission du Congo* [The Needs of the Congo Mission]." He began to scan its contents. Then he read it word for word.

It told of the need for medical missionaries far up the Ogowe River in French Equatorial Africa. This opportunity captured his imagination. Writing about this incident years later he said, "The article finished, I quietly began my work. My search was over."

To read those words might lead one to think that the decision was completely spontaneous. On the surface it was. But he had really been preparing for it ever since his boyhood days when his father had read him stories of heroic missionaries and had illustrated his sermons with similar episodes.

He had also been prepared for this job by the vivid experience of seeing Bartholdi's statue of Admiral Braut in the city of Colmar. At the foot of that statue was a young Negro boy, whose sad, penetrating eyes had burned themselves into Schweitzer's mind so that he could never forget them.

The next few years after his decisions to become a doctor were strenuous ones. Had it not been for his strong physique and his sense of purpose, he could not have stood the strain. On Sundays he preached and during the week he lectured to a group of keen, alert students in the theological seminary. Sandwiched in between these two jobs were organ recitals in many parts of Europe, for Schweitzer was already a leading authority on the music of Bach and an expert on organs.

As if this were not enough, he somehow found time to

write a book about Bach in German as a companion volume to an earlier one on the same subject in French. He also completed *The Quest for the Historical Jesus*. Both books were acclaimed as outstanding, and musicians and ministers still read them as standard works in their fields.

Many a night in this period of his life Schweitzer studied with his feet in cold water in order to keep awake. He refers to this period as one of "continual struggle with fatigue."

Despite all these duties, he did not lose sight of his real goal. In October of 1911 he took the state medical examinations and passed them. When he finished them he says he "could now grasp the fact that the terrible strain of the medical courses was now behind me. Again and again I had to assure myself that I was really awake and not dreaming."

A year of medical work as an intern and the writing of his dissertation were the only hurdles between him and the completion of the work for his degree. He cleared both of them easily. For the dissertation he wrote on the medical and mental aspects of the life of Jesus as they related to his spiritual message. This enabled him to combine his interests in medicine and religion. He completed his work for the M.D. degree brilliantly and added this honor to the degrees which he already had in philosophy and religion.

At last he could apply for work as a medical missionary. Naturally he turned to the Paris Missionary Society whose article had stirred him so deeply. He asked them to send him to Africa. They examined his records with great care. Their decision was that he seemed to have the "correct Christian love," but they were not sure that he had the "correct Christian beliefs." Then, too, he was a German citizen with degrees from a German university, and their work was carried on by Frenchmen.

Schweitzer had foreseen these difficulties. As he says, "Anyone who proposes to do good must not expect people to roll stones out of his way, but must accept his lot calmly even if they roll a few more into it."

From the French Colonial Office he obtained approval of his German diploma.

Then he promised to remain "mute as a fish" so far as preaching was concerned. Remaining silent had been a part of his intention when he decided to go to Africa. As he says, "I wanted to be a doctor that I might be able to work without having to talk. For years I had been giving myself out in words, and it was with joy that I had followed the calling of theological teacher and of preacher. But this new form of activity I could not represent to myself as being talking about the religion of love but only as actually putting it into practice."

As to language and citizenship, he had been born and brought up in Alsace, that section between France and Germany which had shifted back and forth with the various peace treaties between the two nations. It was merely an accident of history and geography that Alsace had become German in 1870, five years before his birth. After all, his parents had been French and he knew that language as well as German.

Eventually he was accepted. After a brief but intensive study in Paris of tropical medicine, he was almost ready to leave for his post.

Money was badly needed for this work, so he gave a series of concerts. Among them was a benefit arranged by his friends in the Paris Bach Society, which he had helped to organize.

The professors and students at Strasbourg University contributed liberally to his funds. And many of his former colleagues and students collected money from their churches and friends. Schweitzer did not like to "beg money," but he even welcomed visits to solicit funds because the pleasant associations they brought outnumbered the unpleasant ones.

There were supplies to be assembled, too. It was not easy for an intellectual and an artist to adjust himself to the minute details involved in ordering and packing supplies to equip a hospital in Africa. But he soon accustomed himself to this new work and even found "artistic satisfaction" in preparing the lists of things needed. Before he left there were seventy crates of supplies assembled for the journey.

On Good Friday, 1913, Schweitzer and his wife said good-by to his family and friends in the little town of Günsbach in Alsace, where Albert had spent his childhood and youth. They traveled on to Strasbourg and then to Paris.

On Easter Sunday they attended the St. Sulpice Church. That was a particularly appropriate farewell, for the famous Charles Marie Widor played the organ there. Just twenty years before that time young Albert Schweitzer had started taking lessons from that well-known musician. Ordinarily his fees for such lessons were high. But he had not charged Albert a single franc. As soon as he had heard him play and knew that he came from a poor preacher's family, he took him on as a special pupil. He had been fascinated by the fact that the boy had begun playing the old square piano in his own home at the age of five, that he had begun to play the church organ in Günsbach at the age of eight when his feet could scarcely reach the pedals, and that he had begun to substitute as church organist at the age of nine. Widor had seen real talent in this young man and had been his enthusiastic teacher and faithful friend for many years. Now, on this Easter Sunday, he was to say farewell to his most brilliant pupil. With what mixed emotions they must have parted.

Soon Albert Schweitzer and his wife were on their way to Africa. They sailed from Bordeaux and first touched Africa at Dakar. From there they went on a little farther until they reached the mouth of the Ogooué River. There they changed to a smaller boat and began to push into the interior.

At last they reached their destination—Lambaréné, in French Africa, only a few miles from the equator. The place where they were to live was in a low, damp country, filled with giant trees and luxuriant foliage. It was a hot, humid country—one of the most unhealthy spots in the world. The nights were like the days, so there was no relief even when one slept. Very few Europeans could endure the climate longer than a few months before fatigue and anemia forced them to a better climate to recuperate.

It was also a sparsely settled country. Its inhabitants were the remnants of eight powerful tribes which had been killed off by the twin evils which the white men had introduced—alcohol and the slave trade. Disease had also taken a terrific toll.

Cannibalism was also still in existence in that part of the world, and the word "missing" was often a synonym for "eaten."

Furthermore, it was a country where food was scarce. Cows could not be kept here. Potatoes and peas could not be grown in such a climate. Even such staples as flour and rice had to be imported. True, there was lots of fruit, but people needed more than fruit to be healthy.

As soon as they arrived the Schweitzers discovered the difficulties in equipment and labor with which they would have to contend. They had expected to find a small building of corrugated iron as an office, but a boom in the timber country had attracted the men who were supposed to have erected this building. Consequently they had to use an old henhouse for a consulting room and do much of their work out of doors under the penetrating rays of the tropical sun.

It was not until fall that they were able to get enough help to build a small building 26 by 13 feet, with iron walls and a palm tree roof. This served as a dispensary, consulting room, and operating room.

In the process of building it, Dr. Schweitzer had to supervise the work and help a great deal himself. Otherwise it would not have been built properly or at all. He learned, too, that money is less meaningful in tropical Africa than in Europe. People in the tropics did not have the incentive to work feverishly, partly because of the climate and partly because of the conditions of life there.

Schweitzer had come as a medical missionary and there was certainly need for him. One of the natives was right when he remarked, "Here among us everybody is ill." Some were the victims of malaria and swamp fever. Many suffered from dysentery. A large number had sores and ulcers. Others were cursed with hernia. Leprosy and sleeping sickness were fairly common and rheumatism much more frequent than in Europe. Many had been mauled by hippopotamuses. To further plague them there was the tsetse fly, "compared with which the worst mosquito is a comparatively harmless crea-ture," according to the doctor. At least there was some consola-tion in the fact that cancer and appendicitis were unknown!

As soon as Schweitzer had won the confidence of the local people, they flocked to him. They came long distances on foot or in canoes to visit the *oganga*, or fetish man, as they called him. Albert Schweitzer, M.D., was hardly a fetish man, but the natives assumed that he who cures can also cause disease.

The fact that he could help so many people was a source of tremendous satisfaction to Schweitzer. He had spent the first twenty years of his life "getting." Now he was "giving." The satisfaction of the latter far surpassed the former. "Just to see the joy of those who are plagued with sores, when these have been cleanly bandaged up and they no longer have to drag their poor, bleeding feet through the mud, makes it worthwhile to work here," he said.

He was acutely sensitive to the needs of each patient, even though he sometimes had to hurry through a medical examina-tion because there were so many people who needed his atten-tion. It is not surprising that he was so sensitive, however. He had been so ever since he was a boy. A typical story of his sensitivity even as a child is told in his *Memoirs of Childhood and Youth*. In his early days at school he had taken on one of the bigger boys in a fight. It looked for a time as if Albert would be beaten, but he finally succeeded in pinning the boy to the ground. As his opponent lay there gasping for breath, he said, "If I had broth—every day—the way you do—I could throw you down—too." From then on Albert disliked soup and insisted on eating small meals because he did not want to be different from the other boys.

His family had also had an overcoat made for him, but Albert had refused to wear it. Many of the other boys did not have winter coats and he did not want to wear one when they went without.

So it was hard for him to work in such primitive conditions and to give only a little time to each patient. But that was all he could do, so he made the most of it.

Fortunately he had a wonderful helper in his wife, Helene. He had met her at the University of Strasbourg when she was studying to be a teacher. She, too, had dreams about some special service to humanity and they had planned together over the years. When Albert Schweitzer decided to become a doctor and go to Africa, she had taken up nursing in order to be a help to him in his work.

So as he worked in the tiny hospital in the jungle she was always by his side or near by helping him in every possible way.

The third member of the trio in those early months was Joseph Azvawami. Joseph was a native who could neither read nor write, but he knew eight African dialects as well as English and French and could act as an interpreter. He could not read the labels on the bottles, but he remembered how they looked and where they belonged, and could help in that way, too. Without the companionship and expert help of his wife and the devoted service of his man "Friday," this medical Robinson Crusoe would have been greatly handicapped.

In a few cases Schweitzer took people into the hospital or dispensary without any fee. But he tried as much as possible to get them to make a payment of some kind. What it was or how much mattered very little. It was the principle that he wanted to establish.

Sometimes he received money. More often he would be given chickens, eggs, or bananas. At first this rule requiring patients to contribute to the hospital was difficult to enforce. Many patients clung to the local custom of expecting a gift as a token of a new friendship instead of giving something. Gradually, however, the new custom was accepted, even though it was not always strictly carried out by everyone.

In this way he helped to build up a feeling of interest in the hospital and a sense of responsibility to it on the part of patients.

When Dr. Schweitzer had made his decision to go to Africa, he had given up three things. He had given up his music, his preaching, and his teaching. His friends in the Paris Bach Society had sent him a specially constructed piano with a zinc cover for protection against the elements and special pedals which made it something like an organ. For months he did not play on this instrument. He was busy with his medical work and the construction of new buildings for his rapidly growing practice. He felt, too, that if he began to play on this piano, he might want to go back to Europe. So, rather than be tempted, he refused to play.

One evening after a very difficult day he finally decided to play the piano-organ. It was the only way he could find to relax. Besides, why shouldn't he use his spare time to perfect his technique and better acquaint himself with the music of the masters. Someday he would need to go back to Europe to raise funds for the hospital. If he kept in practice, he could perhaps give concerts and raise money for his work in Africa.

From that time on he would often sit down after a hard day's work and play for hours at a time. He would be tired when he was through, but he would be mentally refreshed. At other times he would sit up late at night and write about Bach for a series of three volumes that an American publisher had requested.

As time moved along he was cordially accepted by the other missionaries in that section of Africa. They asked that the ban be lifted on his preaching. Scarcely anything could have pleased him more. He had won the confidence of his colleagues. And now he could preach through words as well as through deeds.

This did not conflict with his earlier resolve, however. He had proved in practice the things about which he would preach. These two forms of ministry could now go on simultaneously.

So on Sundays services were held in the hospital or out of doors under the trees with Albert Schweitzer, D.D., in charge. After a musical prelude on the victrola, he would speak to the natives. He would speak as simply as possible, using illustrations from daily life to explain his ideas. A few points he would make over and over. As he states it, "If anybody after a stay at the hospital takes away with him even three or four simple sayings which give him something to think about, it is already a great thing for his life."

These short talks would be given in French and Joseph would translate them into Pahouin and Bendjabis, the two most commonly used dialects.

A short prayer, an organ postlude, and the service would be over.

Dr. Schweitzer and his wife had planned to return to Europe sometime in 1914 for a short vacation, but the opening of World War I changed their plans. At first the Schweitzers were made prisoners in their own home, since they were Germans living in French territory. The natives insisted upon seeing them, however, and the rule soon had to be relaxed.

Part of the time in these early months of partial imprisonment they lived on the coast. When the tide was in, the doctor helped the natives roll logs onto the beach. When the tide was out he saw patients and worked on the first volume in a series of books entitled *The Philosophy of Civilization*.

All through these years he had been diagnosing the ills of human beings. He had also been diagnosing the ills of society. As he saw it, there had been a "growth of a peculiar intellectual and spiritual fatigue in this generation." He wanted to probe its causes and its remedies.

As he thought about the sad condition of the world, he decided that "in our mental and spiritual life we are not only below the level of past generations, but are in many respects only living on their achievements." He feared that "not a little of this heritage was beginning to melt away in our hands."

Out of months of wrestling with the problem of the decline of civilization came some positive ideas as to ways in which this slide down the toboggan could be prevented. He decided that men had become too concerned about their own comforts and conveniences. They were *realists*—absorbed in the present. It seemed to him that people needed again to become *idealists*, interested in the welfare of the whole world. People everywhere needed to develop "a world view" and to think about the kind of world they would like to create. To achieve such goals men and women would need the "will to peace."

In those days there was a battle royal going on between

Christianity and science. Schweitzer saw no reason for such a conflict. He was a Christian and a scientist and saw no reason why others could not be. As he thought about the Christians he had met, he decided that too many of them had emphasized feeling to the exclusion of thinking. He considered such a renunciation of thinking as a kind of "spiritual bankruptcy." "Christianity," he said, "cannot take the place of thinking, but it must be founded on it."

The doctor was trying to look at the world through regular glasses instead of through rose-tinted ones. People often accused him of being a pessimist. His answer was that "my knowledge is pessimistic, but my willing and hoping are optimistic. . . . Because I have confidence in the power of truth and of the spirit, I believe in the future of mankind."

He was writing out such thoughts as these when word came that he and his wife were to be sent to an internment camp in France as war prisoners. Quickly he handed the incomplete manuscript to an American missionary friend and jotted down notes in French on what he had written. He wrote these notes under headings which made them look like a history of the Renaissance in order to pass any disagreeable censor. Throughout the war he was to continue working on this project and it was eventually published in 1923 under the title, *The Decay and Restoration of Civilization.*

In the camp at Garaison in the Pyrenees and later in another camp at St.-Rémy in Province, the Schweitzers were interned with people from all over the world. From them the doctor says that he learned much. Soon he was at work helping the camp doctor. He served as an assistant, even though he knew much more than the man in charge.

There was no organ on which he could practice, but he and his friends built a table and marked out keys on it. Then he marked out pedals on the floor. It was a poor substitute, but it was better than nothing. On this make-believe organ he practiced many hours.

Towards the end of the war he and Mrs. Schweitzer were sent to Germany in an exchange of prisoners. Once again he found himself in Strasbourg, where he had studied and then taught and preached. He found work there in a municipal hospital as a doctor and in the St. Nicholas church as a preacher. So life went on despite a world war.

To his parents, however, life was harsher. In 1916 his mother had been run down by cavalry horses and killed. His father had stayed on in the little town of Günsbach at great risk in order to be with his parishioners. In spite of difficulties, Albert made his way to him as soon as possible. He tried to persuade his father to leave this dangerous center of fighting, but he would not leave.

Finally the war came to an end and Dr. Schweitzer could take part once again in world events. An invitation came from Sweden in 1920 to lecture at the University of Uppsala. He accepted. There he regained his health, which had been seriously impaired by the years in Africa and by the months of internment.

There he also started work on a book which was to be called *On the Edge of the Primeval Forest*. This was the story of his early years in Africa and was a thrilling tale. Soon it was translated into German, Dutch, English, Danish, Swedish and Finnish.

While in Sweden he also went on a concert tour which won

him new support for his work in Lambaréné. Other concert tours followed in Switzerland, Denmark, Czechoslovakia, Spain, and England. With the proceeds from these concerts he paid off his debts and had enough funds to return to Africa in 1924.

Before sailing, he somehow found time to complete the volumes in his *History of Civilization*, to write a book on *Christianity and the Religions of the World*, and a tiny volume called *Memoirs of Childhood and Youth*.

When he returned to his hospital, he found the building in which he had stored his belongings still standing. But the wilderness had overrun almost everything else. Fortunately he had designed a small hospital ward of corrugated iron which had been sent in sections to Africa. That helped some. With him was a young doctor from England, and that relieved Dr. Schweitzer, too.

Nevertheless there was plenty to do. He decided to devote his mornings to being a doctor and his afternoons to being a builder. Soon the jungle hospital was fuctioning as before, only on a larger scale. Word of his work had spread throughout Europe and he was beginning to get help of various kinds. One of the most useful gifts was a small motorboat from The Friends of Lambaréné in Sweden. This saved him many hours of time in getting to patients in outlying districts and also helped him to save his energy. Helpers began to come to Africa, too. Some were doctors and some were nurses, most of them from Switzerland, but some from other countries.

During the late 1920s and early 1930s he made several trips to Europe to lecture and give organ recitals. On these trips he would shut himself away from the world for a time and write.

In this period he produced *The Mysticism of the Apostle Paul* and *Out of My Life and Thought,* which was another book about his life.

Universities vied with each other to honor him with degrees and to tempt him with offers of professorships. But no one could lure him back to Europe permanently. These were only visits; one could scarcely call them vacations.

Each time he returned to Africa to help to atone "for the terrible sufferings which we white people have been bringing upon them [the native Negroes] ever since the day on which the first of our ships found its way to their shores."

In 1939 the doctor set out again for Europe. He was disturbed by the reports which he had been receiving about conditions in Germany, but he did not know how near another world war was until he reached France. When he disembarked at Bordeaux, read the papers, and talked to his friends, he decided that he would remain only a few days. He ordered supplies for the hospital, consulted with some of his supporters, took care of his personal affairs—and within twelve days he was on his way back to Lambaréné.

War did break out soon and Schweitzer was glad that he was back in Africa. If he had stayed much longer in Europe, he might have been caught there for the remainder of the war.

During this great world conflict the jungle hospital stayed open and Dr. Schweitzer was always there on duty. But the war made the work much more difficult than before. It was almost impossible to get medical supplies or food from Europe. Finally a boatload of drugs and provisions was sent from Switzerland. But the boat was torpedoed and everything was lost.

A good many Europeans were stranded in the interior of French Equatorial Africa and many of them became ill. Off they would go to Schweitzer's hospital, thus adding further to its burdens.

Lambaréné seemed a long way off from the main theaters of World War II. But it did not escape the fighting. During October and November, 1940, the troops of General de Gaulle and those of the Vichyites were struggling for the control of French Equatorial Africa. They were fighting within a short distance of Lambaréné. In fact they came so close that Schweitzer had special corrugated iron sidings added to all the wooden buildings as a special protection.

Fortunately, however, both sides agreed to leave the hospital unharmed.

A military road was needed about this time, and soon the jungle saw for the first time the giant road-making machines which tore their way through the virgin timber. This road had one special advantage for the Jungle Doctor. Mrs. Schweitzer had not been well during these past few years and she had spent a good bit of her time in Europe, living part of the time with their married daughter in Switzerland. She had been caught by the war and had had difficulty in getting back to Lambaréné. This road did shorten her journey once she reached Africa, for it ran directly from Algiers to Lambaréné. Schweitzer estimates that it saved her three months of traveling at that time.

His greatest concern in this period was the food supply. Fortunately he had stored up a three-year supply of rice. That helped a lot. Then he collected a much needed supply of fats from the oil palms on the plantation. The garden was gradually slipping into the river, and he arranged for a retaining wall to be built around it.

Friends in the United States finally succeeded in getting a consignment of medicines to him in 1942, and his English friends managed to send some supplies in 1943. From the United States, England, and Switzerland he also obtained iron and liver extract for the treatment of anemia. He also got some sulphonamide for the treatment of the ever prevalent ulcers. For the cure of tetanus he substituted magnesium sulphate and morphine, luminal, and chloral hydrate for the antitetanus which had become too old to be useful.

It was a lonely time for the Schweitzers and their co-workers. But they were not forgotten by their friends abroad. On the doctor's seventieth birthday, January 14, 1945, the British Broadcasting Company told the story of the Jungle Doctor and played recordings of his organ recitals. In isolated Lambaréné the doctor was able to hear the birthday celebration and to know that he had friends in war-torn England as well as elsewhere.

By 1948 Albert Schweitzer was ready to return to Europe after nearly twelve years in the oppressive climate of central Africa, working under terrific pressure. He returned to his home at Günsbach for a short rest. Then he plunged into the further writing of the third volume in his *Philosophy of Civilization*.

This volume, like its predecessors, would stress the idea of "reverence for life." Those three words are a brief summary of the philosophy which Schweitzer had developed over the years in trying to find an ideal by which the world could recover its sanity.

According to him, "anyone who has accustomed himself to regard the life of any living creature as worthless is in danger of arriving also at the idea of worthless human lives—the idea which is playing so disastrous a part in the thought of our time." Writing further about this idea, Schweitzer said, "We have no right to inflict suffering and death on another living creature unless there is some unavoidable necessity for it, and we ought all of us to feel what a horrible thing it is to cause suffering and death out of mere thoughtlessness."

He felt that if a person considered all life—insect, animal, and human—sacred, people would begin to treat one another differently. Life in all its forms would then become something important and worth respecting, rather than cheap and easily destroyed.

It was a simple philosophy but, like a good many simple things, very difficult to live out.

Many people in the United States had long wanted to see Schweitzer. They had tried to get him to visit the United States, but he had stayed on in Africa. Finally, in 1949, he accepted an invitation to attend the 200th anniversary of the birth of the great German, Goethe, which was being celebrated in Aspen, Colorado.

When his boat docked in New York City, a crowd of newspapermen and photographers were on hand to catch a glimpse of the world-famous man. They found this large person with the shaggy mustache and unruly gray hair a most friendly person. He was not used to the procedures of American newspapermen, but willingly posed for pictures. When his interpreter told him that they wanted a picture of him with the skyline of New York in back of him, he smiled and said "*Mais oui, New York et moi!* [Oh yes, New York and I.]"

All through his life he had studied Goethe and had gained much from the thinking of this world-minded poet and writer. In 1927 the city of Frankfurt, the birthplace of Goethe, had awarded Schweitzer the annual prize for the person who had rendered the most outstanding service to society and who had reflected the many-sidedness which characterized Goethe. Then in 1932 Frankfurt had called Schweitzer to deliver the oration at the time of the 100th anniversary of the death of Goethe.

It was particularly appropriate that he should make the main address at the Goethe celebration in 1949 in the United States. He gave this lecture twice, once in French and once in German, with translations in English, pointing out that Goethe was a keen observer of the evil in man and in society. But he stressed the fact that Goethe also had a profound belief in the ability of men and women to master their own destiny. Uppermost in his mind was the idea of doing good for the pure love of good rather than for personal gain.

In a special interview he outlined his own philosophy in very simple terms. "What the world lacks most," he said, "is men who occupy themselves with the needs of other men. In this unselfish labor a blessing falls on both the helper and the helped. . . . Our greatest mistake as individuals is that we walk through life with closed eyes and do not notice our chances. As soon as we open our eyes and deliberately search, we see many who need help—not in big things, but in the littlest things. Wherever a man turns he can find someone who needs him."

This simple service to others he called the "second job" of everyone. "Organized welfare work is of course necessary," he said, "but the gaps must be filled by personal service performed with loving kindness."

Schweitzer did not stay long in the United States. But while he was here he spent a good deal of his time talking to doctors and research workers about the latest findings in medicine. He was particularly glad to take back with him some of the latest drugs for the control of leprosy. These he would use in the jungle hospital.

Three weeks was not long enough for many people to see or hear the doctor. But many people heard for the first time the story of one of the great men of our times, the story of the man who had become one of the world's outstanding philosophers, the world's greatest authority on the music of Johann Sebastian Bach, one of the pioneers in tropical medicine, and a great humanitarian. Whenever they thought of Africa, they would think of Albert Schweitzer, the Jungle Doctor.

SUN YAT-SEN

Creator of Modern China

On a summer day in 1883 a small ship neared the island of Cap Suy Mun in the harbor of Hong Kong, China. As the boat neared the port the captain called the passengers together to remind them that they should get their gifts ready for the customs officials who would soon be coming on board.

No one seemed to object to this announcement. It was assumed that the black-gowned officials with their silver belts and swords would swoop down like vultures and collect whatever they could from the passengers. This was the ordinary procedure and it was accepted as a necessary evil in the China of those days.

As soon as the ship was moored, the officials came on board, collected their gifts, and went ashore. Then a second set of officials arrived and demanded their levy, or "likin"—a tax originally used to suppress rebellion. The passengers dug a little deeper and came up with more gifts, or graft. No sooner had they disappeared than a third set of men appeared to demand a duty on opium. They, too, received what they asked. The boat was ready to sail when a fourth group clambered on board to extort payment on the petroleum in the ship.

Over in the corner a young Chinese had been observing this parade of extortionists with disgust and then anger. As one

group after another demanded payment, his anger rose. His fists became tighter and tighter. His sensitive mouth grew firmer and firmer.

This was an outrage, a disgrace to his country and his countrymen. Why were all these people so docile? How many times would they submit to this violation of their rights? Were they helpless before the representatives of the Manchus?

By now he was mad. He broke his silence and spoke angrily against these corrupt agents of a monarch who was exploiting the Chinese. Of course he knew that such customs had been carried on in China ever since they had been conquered by their northern neighbors, the Manchus, in the middle of the seventeenth century. But that did not make such customs right. It was time that people protested, even if it meant taking risks.

The young man with the stocky body, the high forehead, the dark hair, and the sensitive mouth became the center of attention. How foolish of him to fight, the other peasants said. How unwise to protest.

The officials moved over to him, seized him, and told him to open his baggage. He refused. The captain of the boat pled with him to be quiet and to do what they demanded. But he could not be stopped.

As a result of his conduct the officials swore out a warrant against the captain and prevented the ship from sailing until the next day. They did not take young Sun Yat-sen captive. After all, he was just a rebellious young man who hadn't yet learned the way things were done. They did take most of his possessions. That should teach him a lesson!

Arriving home this young upstart caused further trouble.

Soon after his return there was a special festival in the village. Everyone assembled on that day at the temple to pay their respects to the gods.

Sun Yat-sen thought all this was silly. Why should they bother to pay homage to worship these gods? After all, these statues were only idols and he was not going to be fooled by them.

So the brash seventeen-year-old climbed up on a pedestal and told his fellow townsmen how foolish they were. And while they stood dumfounded by this rash talk, he moved over to the statue and broke off one of the god's arms.

As if this were not enough, he criticized the practice of concubinage, denounced the smoking of opium, railed against foot-binding, and laughed at the people who thought the Emperor was Chinese rather than a foreigner.

No one had ever talked this way in Choyhung and the people were enraged. Some demanded his head. Others said he should be buried alive in a pit. A few were ready to tear him limb from limb.

The elders held them back. The boy's father was a quiet, honest peasant and much respected in the village. His family was honorable. The boy must be mad. Or perhaps he had picked up some of his ideas from missionaries and foreigners and didn't know what he was saying.

The decision was made to banish him from his home town. That would be a real punishment to a Chinese. It would be a kind of living death.

Little did they know that they were banishing a boy who would later become the father of modern China and a great world figure. They only knew that he had gone against the customs of his day and that he must be taught a hard lesson. It would have taken greater foresight than any of them had to know what was in store for young Sun Yat-sen. They had better hindsight, and this is what they had seen.

This rebel had been born on November 12, 1866, in their village of Choyhung. This was in the southeastern tip of China, forty miles south of Canton and thirty miles north of Macao. It was an ordinary little Chinese village of bamboo and mortar houses. Surrounding it were the rice fields which stretched as far as the eye could see. Here also were kingfishers, with their blue feathers which were exported to Peking, and the blue reeds which were sent off to the nearest city. From these reeds and feathers came the name of the town, Choyhung, or Blue Thriving Village.

The house where Yat-sen had spent his boyhood was a typical building made of mud and lime mixed with rice straw. The floor was made of beaten earth. In the house were some tables and wooden beds.

As a boy Yat-sen flew kites, spun tops, set off firecrackers on special days, kicked feathers, and played leapfrog. He worked in the rice fields to help earn the living for the family of eight— his father and mother, two brothers, three sisters, and himself.

Occasionally he had the treat of listening to the tales of an old soldier who had fought in the Taiping rebellion against the Emperor. But most of the time life went on in the same way that it had gone on in Choyhung for centuries. It was a quiet, happy life, upset once in a while by the raids of Manchu soldiers.

One special feature of Choyhung was its school. Boys and girls in China were not supposed to go to school together, but the school here was coeducational. There Sun Yat-sen studied seven days a week, with only a day off once in a long time for a local holiday.

Even as a school boy he had shown signs of independence. Day after day the children chanted their lessons out loud. Everything had to be memorized and this was the way to learn things by heart. But Sun Yat-sen didn't see any sense to all the things they had to learn. He told the teacher he thought that all this memorizing was "nonsense."

Of course such insolence and rebellion could not be tolerated. Imagine calling the classics of Confucius and Mencius "nonsense." They were the sacred words of the sages of China and were not to be challenged—or even explained—in the schools of those days. So young Sun Yat-sen was severely punished.

This happy, uneventful life was interrupted by the return of Yat-sen's brother Ah Mei. This was a great event in the family, for he had been living in Hawaii, or the Sandalwood Mountains, as those islands were called in southern China.

Stirred by stories of Hawaii, Yat-sen begged to go back with his brother. This was to be the beginning of a new life for this Chinese lad. It was to make him dissastisfied with existence as he had known it and to lead to such events as we have described earlier in this chapter.

When he first reached Hawaii, he lived with his brother and worked in the rice fields and in a store which his brother ran in the Pearl Harbor area. But soon he was enrolled in a mission school in Honolulu run by the Anglican Church.

There he learned English, read and studied the Bible, was baptized, and won a scholarship when he graduated in 1882—

a prize consisting of a book on missionary life in China and a pigskin Bible, presented by the Dowager Queen of the island.

There he also learned geography. At least he learned the geography of the British Empire. That was a widening experience, for the Manchus had not allowed the geography of anything but China to be taught, for fear that the people would be corrupted by learning about the rest of the world.

In Hawaii Sun Yat-sen had also seen democratic customs beginning to appear in that mid-Pacific island. He had likewise seen something of Christianity—although not always in its best form.

All these experiences became a part of him. He had picked up new ideas and was in revolt against the kind of life he had known as a child. These new ideas were churning around in his mind when he returned to China in 1883 to find a wife. All this helps to explain his action at Cap Suy Mun in the harbor of Hong Kong and at the village festival in Choyhung.

After he was banished from his home town, he made his way to Hong Kong. What he did there during the next few months, no one knows. In later life he never elaborated on that period of his life.

We do know that in 1884 he enrolled in Queen's College and shortly after that he was married.

Even more important to him were some political events during those two years of 1883–84. It was then that the French attacked the Chinese government of the Manchus and succeeded in winning the territory of Annam. The Manchus were disliked by the Chinese in the South because they were considered foreigners from the North. But up until now they had been respected and feared. They were considered clever and invincible—until the French proved otherwise.

Like many other young men, Sun Yat-sen saw that the Manchus could be beaten. True, it had been Europeans that had proved their weakness. But if the Europeans could defeat them, why couldn't the Chinese? This was the beginning of his determination to become a revolutionary, of his resolve to free China from "foreign" rule. This was the beginning of a new life.

No sooner had he begun to think in these terms than he heard from his brother in Hawaii. Ah Mei pled with him to come back to help settle up some financial matters for the family. The real purpose of his invitation to Yat-sen, however, was to get him away from Hong Kong, where he had begun to take part in revolutionary activities. Also Ah Mei hoped to persuade him to give up Christianity.

But the older brother's plot failed. When Yat-sen discovered the real purpose behind the invitation to Hawaii, he would not give in. His brother threatened to cut off his family inheritance. But that did not work, either. "Money will never make me betray Christianity," he declared. "Indeed, money is a curse to China, a source of corruption, and a burden to the people."

He remained a Christian and a revolutionary.

His friends now expected him to become a missionary. He did, but his "mission" was different from the one he had expected. It was to free China from control by the nations of western Europe and by the Manchus, to restore her faith in her future as well as her pride in her past, to unify and democratize this sprawling nation of over four hundred million persons, and to earn for her an important place in the family of nations.

Sun Yat-sen had no funds with which to carry on this special mission, so he decided to earn his living as a doctor and to continue his activities to free China on the side.

He studied first at the Victoria Hospital in Hong Kong, then at the Pok Tsai Hospital in Canton, and finally at the Alice Memorial Hospital in Hong Kong. In 1892 he graduated as a physician.

The next few years were difficult ones for this young doctor. As he described them later, they were "like one day in my hard fight for national liberty, and my medical practice was no more to me than a means to introduce my propaganda to the world."

For a time he worked in Macao, because the Portuguese were in control there and it was a safe base. Then the Chinese brought pressure on the Portuguese, and Yat-sen had to escape. He moved on to Canton for a time, but an insurrection in which he was a leader failed, and he could not stay there.

Now he became a world wanderer. The first attempts of the rebels had proved that it was necessary to have adequate funds, adequate supplies, adequate recruits, and adequate plans. They needed support from other sources, and he now set off to enlist others in their movement.

In 1895 he went to Japan and then on to Hawaii. From there he crossed the Pacific to the United States. Then he crossed the continent and traveled on to England.

Everywhere he went he met small groups of Chinese emigrants—gardeners, small merchants, laundrymen, restaurant keepers, sailors. With them he shared his dream of a free China which would play a leading role in the world, of throwing off the control of China by Western European nations, of China leading the rest of Asia to independence—and eventually to peace and justice.

These groups were small, but he began to organize them into secret societies, such as the Hsing Chung Hui—the Association for the Regeneration of China. These men and woman had had similar experiences to his. They knew that there was nothing about people in the Western world which the Chinese could not copy. They knew that freedom was possible for their fatherland.

Everywhere that Sun Yat-sen went he also took the flag which he hoped China would someday fly over her own vast territory as a symbol of nationalism. Its blue was to represent liberty, its white equality, and its red fraternity. The white sun in the center was intended to show China radiating light throughout the world. The twelve rays of the sun symbolized the twelve hours of the day and the twelve hours of the night.

He also took with him a declaration of independence which he shared with these small groups of Chinese which he brought together in different parts of the world. Translated, it says:

> No longer shall we reverence the throne.
> The Son of Heaven is incompetent.
> His officers are corrupt.
> His rule is an abomination.
> He shall give way to the will of the people.
> No longer shall we reverence the throne.

Sun Yat-sen was anxious to shake the faith of the people in the Emperor. But he knew that he must do that slowly. After centuries of belief in this ruler, the people would be slow to accept the idea of overthrowing him. He cast about for a slogan which would express his ideas. Finally he hit upon the phrase, "*Tien Ming Wu Chang*," which means, "Divine right does not last forever."

That would introduce the idea of independence. But it would introduce it slowly. He was wise in knowing his own people well and in planning his strategy for Chinese independence on his intimate knowledge of their ways of thinking and acting.

Here and there he found loyal followers. Typical of the devotion of some of them was the laundryman in Philadelphia who came to him anonymously and dumped his laundry bag full of life savings onto Dr. Sun's bed—and departed.

But these were years of loneliness and discouragement. Later he admitted that "the years between 1895 and 1900 were the most difficult times in the progress of the revolution."

They were exciting, dangerous times, too.

One of the most dangerous experiences in this period took place in London in 1896. It was early on Sunday morning and Yat-sen was on the way to see his friends, the Cantlies, whom he had met as a student in China. They planned to go together to the famous church, St. Martins-in-the-Fields. As he was walking along he was accosted by another Chinese who inquired about Yat-sen's nationality. Striking up a conversation with Dr. Sun, the stranger moved quickly along the street until they were joined by a third Chinese.

Before Sun Yat-sen knew what was happening, he found himself flanked by these two men. They invited him to go to their house, and when he declined their invitation they forced him to go with them.

Once inside, they shut the door and dragged him into a third story room. There he was a prisoner.

Gradually he realized that this was the Chinese Legation and he had been kidnapped by his fellow countrymen. He tried to contact the outside world by dropping notes out the window, weighted with coins. But that did not work.

After several days he became desperate and began to pray. In that way he found calm and new confidence. Then he began to think about other possible ways of escape.

There was an English servant who waited on him, and Yat-sen decided to appeal to him. The boy eventually agreed to take a note to the Cantlies telling them where their Chinese friend had been "jailed."

The Cantlies appealed to Scotland Yard. But the police were not interested in the case. The man involved was Chinese and he was now in the Legation. Since the land on which embassies and legations are housed is always considered "foreign territory," they could not intervene.

The British Foreign Office felt the same way. An attempt was made to print an article about the kidnapping in the London *Times*, but the newspaper officials were not interested, either.

Finally the Cantlies persuaded the London *Globe* to print a front-page interview on the kidnapping of the Chinese revolutionary. This led to pressure by the British Foreign Office to let Sun Yat-sen go. He had become a *cause célèbre* and the Manchus released him.

Dr. Sun now set off on a tour of Europe, but no longer as an inconspicuous Chinese. He was world-renowned.

It was on this European trip among Chinese student groups that he formulated his now famous "*San Min Chu I*," or "Three Principles of the People." This was the core of his plans for modern China. They were not written down for several years, but he began using them in talks and discussions.

The first principle he laid down was *national independence*. Pointing to the examples of the United States of America and Switzerland, Dr. Sun argued that a unified nation could be developed from different kinds of people. In a similar manner "the Manchus, Mongols, Tibetans, Tartars, and Chinese should constitute a single powerful nation." Such a nation would also be free to govern itself rather than be run by Westerners.

To win national independence demanded the second principle—democracy. According to Dr. Sun, everyone in China should have the right to vote, to recall their elected representatives when the people were dissatisfied with them, to reject laws through popular referendums, and to propose or draft laws by means of the direct initiative of the citizens. In his interpretation of democracy he was obviously influenced by the ideas of initiative, referendum, and recall which were being discussed widely in the United States at that time.

These first two principles had to be based on a third—*livelihood*. For centuries the Chinese peasants had lived on a very low standard. With the increase of population, this standard had been getting poorer and poorer. Dr. Sun felt that the people must have more and better food, better housing, better clothing. Those were the bare essentials of life.

To obtain a rise in the standard of living for the masses of China would mean a more equitable distribution of land. It would mean the breaking up of the large estates owned by a few wealthy Chinese. It would mean the nationalization of transportation and communication. It would mean the formation of co-operatives. It would mean the introduction of new methods of raising food. It would require wide social and economic reforms.

These were the three principles on which the revolution must be based. Sometimes Dr. Sun summarized them as national independence, democracy, and livelihood. At other times he put them into the phrase: "The people are to have, the people are to rule, the people are to enjoy." They closely resembled the phrase of Lincoln, "Government of the people, by the people, and for the people." He readily admitted the indebtedness to Lincoln for this concise statement of his political, social, and economic philosophy.

His journey took him again to England and to Canada in 1898, to Japan in 1899, and then back to China.

The next few years were turbulent ones. The year 1900 marked the Boxer Rebellion in China, an uprising against foreign domination. In that event Dr. Sun took no part. But he did lead an unsuccessful insurrection in the Kwangtung Province that same year.

The next two years were spent largely in Japan. Then in 1903 he started on a second world tour. On it he visited the United States, Belgium, France, Germany, and Japan. His third and fourth tours took place in 1909 and 1910 and covered much the same territory. On each of these journeys he was gaining more financial support and more followers to help free China from foreign rule.

Time and time again in this period revolutions were started. But each time they failed. There were four such uprisings in 1907, two in 1908, and one in 1910.

Only the dogged determination of Dr. Sun and his followers

kept the movement from collapsing. Only their willingness to sacrifice kept the movement alive.

In each revolution many of the leaders were killed. Some committed suicide because of their despair. Many of the leaders were imprisoned. Hundreds of faithful followers lost their lives in each of these uprisings and hundreds more were put in jail. But the movement went on.

Finally, in October 1911, came the victory for which they had fought so long. This was the culmination of years of struggle. A variety of factors contributed to the success of this particular revolution.

This time there had been sufficient ammunition. Likewise there had been sufficient funds, largely supplied by overseas Chinese. In this uprising the intellectuals and the peasants were united. The propaganda through newspapers, booklets, and plays had had its effect and there was more widespread participation by the populace. Also, there were important allies in the Imperial Army.

Added to these factors for success were the unsettled conditions growing out of the weak regency for the infant prince P'u-i, their dismissal of the powerful and popular Yüan Shih-k'ai, and the anger of the people over the building of railroads with foreign capital and foreign control.

Starting in Hankow on October 9, 1911, the revolutionaries quickly captured Wuchang, Hanyang, and Hankow. The provincial assembly of Hupeh quickly proclaimed its independence from the throne. Within a month thirteen provinces were free from the national government of the Manchus.

On November 7 Yüan Shih-k'ai was appointed premier, and within a few weeks he had ousted the regency and set up his own government in North China. He had also made overtures of peace with the revolutionaries in the South.

By a strange twist of fate Sun Yat-sen was in the United States when all this was happening. Events had moved quicker than he had anticipated and his first news of victory came when he picked up a newspaper in Denver, Colorado. In these accounts he read that he was to be made provisional president of the new Republic as soon as he could return to China.

But Sun Yat-sen had other plans. To him it seemed more important to go to England and France. The new government would need foreign capital and foreign friends. He was one of the few revolutionaries who had such contacts abroad and he must make such contacts count.

He wired his friends in China and set off for England. There he succeeded in cutting off all financial relations between the international bankers and the Manchus. In France he won a similar agreement.

Now he could return to China. He arrived in Shanghai on Christmas Day of 1911. Four days later he was elected Provisional President of the Chinese Republic.

On New Year's day in 1912 he took the oath of office. In it he promised "faithfully to obey the will of the people, to remain loyal to the nation, and to perform [his] duty in the interests of the citizens until the time comes when the Manchu rule is dethroned and the disturbances within the nation have been brought to an end and the Republic has been established as a prominent nation upon the earth, recognized by all other nations."

After 267 years of Manchu rule, China was at last a republic. And Sun Yat-sen was now its first President.

He did not have a united nation behind him, however. The Emperor was still on his throne and Yüan Shih-k'ai was still in control in the North.

Above all else Dr. Sun wanted peace and a unified nation. So he offered the presidency to Yüan Shih-k'ai as soon as the Emperor was dethroned. He also proposed that Nanking be chosen as the capital city.

By February these terms appeared to be met, and Yüan Shih-k'ai was elected President of the National Assembly. Peace seemed assured.

But there was to be no immediate peace. Yüan Shih-k'ai insisted on staying in the North. A group of leaders from the South traveled to Peking to see him and by a curious coincidence—or was it a coincidence?—a riot broke out as soon as they arrived, and stopped as soon as they left. It looked as if he wanted to prove that he needed to stay in the northern part of China. Dr. Sun had withdrawn from politics for a time, but it was obvious that he could not ignore such troubles. So he made a trip to Peking himself.

There the two leaders of the new Republic reached an agreement. Yüan was to become the political head and Sun would work on his pet scheme for building a network of railroads to help unite the four hundred million people living in more than four million square miles of territory. It was an ambitious and important undertaking. It called for the building of seventy-five thousand miles of railroad in the next ten years. It required $3,000,000 of foreign capital. It would employ two million Chinese laborers. It would be one of the biggest steps in the industrialization of that vast nation.

Dr. Sun went to Japan in 1913 to study the railroads of that small island nation, which had already become partly westernized. While he was there an assassination took place which cast further doubts on Yüan Shih-k'ai's democratic beliefs and intentions. The man who was murdered was the candidate of the Kuomintang, or Nationalist Party, for premier. It looked as if the President of the Republic was involved in the plot.

Within five days Yüan had floated a loan with five of the Great Powers without the sanction of the National Assembly. His intentions seemed clear. He intended to rule as a dictator, disregarding the will of the people through their elected representatives.

Dr. Sun hurried back to Shanghai. His mind was made up. Now he would act. On April 9, 1913, he telegraphed the President, "You are betraying your country. I must oppose you in the same way that I opposed the Ch'ing dynasty."

Yüan responded by ousting Dr. Sun as director general of the railroad board. Civil war had begun. The fight between two men, between two sections of China, between two concepts of government was in the open.

In October Yüan formally became President in an election marked by bribery and violence. In January 1914 he dissolved Parliament. And in January 1916 he proclaimed himself Emperor.

The people were now aroused. They had fought to establish a republic and they had ended up with another emperor. They rose against him and he was forced to give up the title and to restore the Republic. On June 6, 1916, he died.

The record of the next few years is one of hostilities and violence between North and South China and of bitter rivalry between leaders of various factions. In September 1917 Sun Yat-sen was chosen Generalissimo of a government located in Canton, in the South. But he remained in power only until May of 1919.

After he had reorganized the Kuomintang, he went into retirement and began writing *The Principles of National Reconstruction* and *The International Development of China*. The first book was to be a restatement of his ideas on how China could be unified. The second book was a plan for the industrialization of China, including fairly detailed plans for improvement in communication and transportation facilities, the construction and improvement of canals, plans for increased food production, and the introduction and strengthening of various industries.

A temporary peace brought him once again to accept a rival for the presidency in 1920. This time he determined to use Canton as a demonstration center of what could happen throughout China. He replaced the walls of the city with modern streets. He built playgrounds and parks for the people. He increased the public utilities of the city. This was local reconstruction. Some day there would be national reconstruction along similar lines.

But his work was hampered by the need to quell rebellions and restore order in one part or another of the struggling Republic.

In all these struggles China had felt alone in the world. She seemed like a small boy surrounded by larger and stronger boys. As Dr. Sun saw his native land, she was the country with the largest population and the oldest continuous culture of any country in the world. But she was also "the poorest and weakest state in the world, occupying the lowest position in international affairs."

As he saw it, "The rest of mankind is the carving knife and the serving dish while we are the fish and the meat." Such a situation was deplorable. As he put it, "Our position now is extremely perilous. If we do not earnestly promote nationalism and weld together our four hundred millions into a strong nation, we face a tragedy—the loss of our country and the destruction of our race."

With those thoughts in mind, he cast about for a friend among the larger powers of the world. Finally he turned to Russia as "the only country that shows signs of helping us."

In 1923 he sent his Chief of Staff, Chiang Kai-shek, to Russia to study their military organization. That same year he invited the Russian, Mikhail Borodin, to come to China as his special personal adviser.

As a result of these and other events, the Chinese army was reorganized, labor unions were encouraged, and the government took a turn to the "left." It is generally agreed that Sun was not a Communist, but there is sharp disagreement on how far he went in his admiration of their system of government, economics, and social life.

Certainly he was profoundly impressed by the way in which the Russians had achieved national independence and the unification of millions of people into one government without the continuous civil wars that raged in China. Possibly he was envious of the way in which Russia had accomplished in a short time what China had been trying to do for a much longer time. But he was certainly critical of the means which they had used and some of the ends which they had achieved.

Before China had really become united, Sun Yat-sen died. His death came on March 12, 1925.

As one looks back on the life of this leader, it is certain that he was a great national leader. He had helped to arouse in the Chinese a spirit of nationalism. He had awakened almost a fifth of the world's population to the great future that could be theirs. He had helped to graft new life onto a centuries-old tree with deep roots in the past. He had awakened the sleeping giant—China. He had showed them that modernization without westernization was possible.

Those contributions alone would not qualify him for selection as a citizen of the world. But he did more than help to free his own people. He helped the millions of members of the yellow race to feel proud of their past, concerned about their present, and optimistic about their future. He helped them to feel that there was a place for them in the modern world—a place of equality with white men, brown men—with everyone. He gave them confidence in themselves.

Conversely, he showed the Western world that China and the whole of Asia could no longer be considered a territory for their imperialism. He made them realize for almost the first time that China and Asia would no longer tolerate the status of colonies. He made them at least partially aware of the fact that a new era had begun in world affairs when each nation would determine for itself its own future.

Is it any wonder that his countrymen should have built a shrine for him on the slopes of the Purple Mountains outside Nanking? Is it any wonder that a ceremonial was introduced in all Chinese schools whereby every Monday morning everyone would sing the national anthem, bow three times before the portrait of Sun Yat-sen, and then repeat some of the famous words of his will? Is it any wonder that Chinese of every political party still honor him and argue as to which side he would take in the bitter quarrels which still tear that vast nation into factions?

Yes, Sun Yat-sen was a rebel against the Manchus and against Western domination in the East. But he was also the creator of modern China. More than that, he was a pioneer in the building of a world community in which all people, regardless of race, class, religion, or nationality, will be free to enjoy the three great principles which he enunciated—national independence, democracy, and a better standard of living for all.

ARTURO TOSCANINI

Maestro of World Music

It was the second evening of the 1886 opera season in Rio
de Janeiro, Brazil, and the hall was crowded. Excited whispers
reverberated around the auditorium. Tension filled the air.
Leopoldo di Miguez, Brazilian conductor and native of Rio,
had shocked his home town by resigning his post after the
opening concert, charging the Italian members of his orchestra
with insubordination and insults.

245

His resignation was deeply resented in Rio. Why should the foreigners in his orchestra ruin the career of a great conductor. His fellow townsmen were at tonight's concert in full force. They intended to cause trouble and revenge the resignation of Miguez.

The lights were lowered. Maestro Superti strode onto the platform and tapped the conductor's stand with his baton. The overture commenced. But no sooner had it begun than a torrent of hisses and shouts poured down upon him. The music could scarcely be heard. Suddenly the music stopped and Superti fled from the orchestra pit.

Backstage the authorities went into a huddle. They implored the chorus master to take over. Not certain whether to face such a violent audience or not, Venturi finally consented. As soon as he stepped onto the stage a cloud of censure burst and he, too, hurried to shelter in the wings.

It looked as if the audience would tolerate no successor to Miguez. But the performance must go on. Desperate, a group of musicians took matters into their own hands and practically forced a nineteen-year-old lad from Parma, Italy, to conduct for them.

As this thin, wiry boy moved to the podium, the audience became quiet. This was something different, something unexpected, something dramatic. A few recognized him as one of the celloists in the orchestra, but most of the audience had no idea who he was.

Toscanini closed the score in front of him, pushed aside the conductor's stand, and raised his baton. The overture recommenced and this time moved on without interruption until the finale.

At the end of the presentation of Aïda, the audience thundered its approval. They had been stunned and pleased by this feat of a hitherto unknown celloist conducting the entire concert from memory—and so well.

The newspaper *Paiz* called the performance "marvelous" and one of the Rio critics said Toscanini was a "conductor of ability, coolness, enthusiasm, and energy."

Such was the sudden rise to fame of Arturo Toscanini, now recognized as a musical genius, as the greatest conductor of this generation, as "the maestro" to a world-wide audience.

Years of undramatic preparation, however, lay behind this rocketlike rise.

Arturo had been born in Parma, Italy, on March 25, 1867. His parents were Claudio and Paola. He was their fourth child and their first son.

Claudio was a tailor by trade and a poor man. He was an ardent admirer and follower of Garibaldi, the military leader who had helped to establish Italy as a modern, independent, united nation. For a short time Claudio had fought under this famous "Sword of Italy." Otherwise he had no claim to fame.

But Claudio and Paola did enjoy music. They saved money to attend the opera as often as possible. When they could not go to the Opera House, they invited a few of their friends to their home and made their own music. Like all small boys, Arturo was troublesome at times, but he was not troublesome on the evenings that there was music. He looked forward to these treats and would inquire when there would be another "concert."

When he was eight, Arturo was sent to school. He did creditable work, but did not shine. At least this was so until he entered the second grade. There he had as his teacher a talented and understanding woman named Signora Vernoni.

To her astonishment Arturo committed to memory the poems and stories which she told, even after he had heard them only once. Signora Vernoni was fascinated by this gift and took a special interest in this quiet boy. She invited him to her house and encouraged him to play the piano. She taught him what she knew and he absorbed this elementary knowledge eagerly.

This wise woman was convinced that the boy had talent. She went to see his parents and tried to persuade them to enroll him in the Parma Conservatory. At first they were reluctant, but eventually they gave in to her request.

Of course Arturo did not have enough background to enter a conservatory, but a local tuba player was hired to prepare him for the entrance examinations. From him Arturo took piano lessons and lessons in harmony and theory. At nine he passed the exams and was admitted to the conservatory.

Life there was severe, but it did not seem to daunt Arturo. He passed up the excursions through the city twice a week and spent all his spare time in the library or in his room. He sold the meat coupons which were given to the students and bought scores with the money. Then he locked himself in his room and wrote out transcriptions of them for the piano.

His fellow students recognized his ability and soon nick-named him *Il Genio*—the genius. He did not like the title, but it stuck.

After two years, Arturo was awarded a scholarship which paid his board and tuition for seven years. Meanwhile his father and mother saved all they could for his other expenses.

On July 14, 1885, he graduated from the Parma Conservatory. His grades in cello, piano, and composition were perfect. He was graduated con *lode distinta*—with the highest distinction.

During the last years at the conservatory he had played in the Parma Royal Theater orchestra and in the Parma Musical Orchestra. But full-time jobs for a young graduate were difficult to find. So when the chance came to go to South America, he took it. It was there that fame came to him.

News of this South American experience did not spread quickly, and for a time Toscanini continued to play the cello in orchestras in Italy. But the singers who had been with him in Rio and elsewhere had not forgotten the brilliant conducting. One of those singers was scheduled to sing in the opera *Edmea* in the city of Turin, and he persuaded the composer, Alfredo Catalani, to let Toscanini conduct.

So on November 4, 1886, Toscanini made his debut as a conductor in his own country. The newspapers had ridiculed the idea of such a young boy conducting. They called him the "beardless bambino" and they pictured him as a little boy with a baton clambering up to the platform to conduct. But after the concert they swallowed their words. They praised him for his memory, for his insight into the compositions, and for his skill as a conductor.

In 1886 and 1887 he toured the smaller cities of Italy with an opera troupe and in 1890 and 1891 he was an assistant conductor in Barcelona, Spain.

His friendship with Catalani had grown during these months and so had Catalani's respect for Toscanini's abilities.

In 1892 he conducted another Catalani opera, *Loreley*, in

Genoa, and later in the year he conducted *La Wally* by the same composer. Later in life, Toscanini showed his respect and admiration for this great man by naming his children after characters in the operas—Wally and Walter.

The year 1892 was the 400th anniversary of the discovery of America by Columbus, and it was an event to be celebrated throughout Italy. Alberto Franchetti, one of the greatest of Italian composers of that day, wrote a special opera for that occasion, entitled *Cristoforo Colombo*. Two performances had been conducted by the great Italian conductor, Luigi Mancinelli. Then he was called to Spain and it looked as if the third performance would have to be called off.

Then someone thought of Toscanini. He was telegraphed and begged to come to Genoa. There were only a few hours before the opening curtain, but he shut himself in his room, studied the score, and conducted it from memory. The performance was acclaimed an outstanding success, and Toscanini's fame spread still further.

In the 1890s Toscanini conducted several "firsts" for contemporary Italian composers, works which today are world famous. One of these was *Pagliacci* by Leoncavallo. Another was *La Bohème* by Puccini.

It was in these days, too, that Toscanini helped to introduce the great operas of Wagner to enthusiastic Italian audiences. On the occasion of the first performance in Italy of *Götterdämmerung*, a special orchestra was brought together in Turin for Toscanini and the event was an outstanding one in the annals of Italian music. In 1897 he presented the first performance of *Tristan and Isolde* and in 1898 *Die Walküre*.

While conducting in Turin, Arturo met a young ballerina

named Carla dei Martini and fell in love with her. In 1897 they were married and she immediately gave up her professional career to devote herself completely to the young and brilliant conductor.

Throughout his life Toscanini was to shatter precedent. This began early. In May of 1898 he was asked to conduct a series of concerts of symphonic music in Turin at the International Exposition. Italians were accustomed to hearing largely the works of Italian composers. But Toscanini wanted them to hear good music, no matter what the nationality of the composer might be. In that series he played more music by Germans than by Italians. There were some who complained. But most people were thrilled by the music under the baton of this rising conductor and were not concerned with the nationality of the composers whose music he chose.

La Scala in Milan was the most famous of all opera houses in the 1890s. It was the mother opera house of the world. When its directors invited Toscanini to become permanent conductor and artistic director there in 1898, he was thrilled. It was the highest honor that could come to a conductor in Italy.

His selection for these posts was the beginning of a lifelong association with La Scala. It was interrupted by long periods abroad, but again and again he returned to this important place. He was there from 1898 until 1903 and again from 1906 until 1908. In 1921, after World War I, he reopened the famed horseshoe-shaped auditorium and from 1921 until 1929 served as its artistic director. In 1929 he celebrated thirty years of association with this mecca of opera lovers. And in 1946 he reopened La Scala after World War II.

At La Scala his programs were varied. There were operas by the great Germans—Wagner and Weber. There were operas by the great Italians, Puccini, Rossini, and Verdi. And there were operas by the Russian Tchaikovsky and the Frenchman Berlioz. Music to him was international and he would play the best of all nations.

There were objections to Toscanini, too, in those years. Some protested against his custom of not playing encores. Some said that he gave too much credit to the composers and did not take the plaudits of the audience with good grace. Some of the musicians complained that he drove them too hard and was intransigent, uncompromising, irreconcilable.

Typical of this latter charge was the case of a soprano who held a note longer than the score indicated. Toscanini cut her short with a quick introduction of the orchestra. To Toscanini she protested, "Maestro, I am the star of this performance." To which he replied curtly, "Madame, the stars are found only in heaven."

Through these early years of conducting Toscanini had been very friendly with Verdi. They understood each other perfectly. They admired each other. The death of Verdi in 1901 was therefore a great personal blow to the young conductor. Four days after the death of the noted composer, Toscanini conducted an all Verdi program with Caruso as one of the soloists. And on the day when his body was taken to its final resting place, Toscanini conducted the chorus which accompanied the cortege. That night he led the performance of *Elisir d'Amore*, and at the end of the opera he conducted the chorus in the rendition of *Nabucco* as a final tribute to his great friend and fellow musician. All through his life Toscanini has played the works of this outstanding composer and has become the world's authority on him.

His troubles at La Scala mounted and in 1903 he left his post in Milan. By now opera companies all over the world were clamoring for him. Everywhere he went he was acclaimed. Critics and composers vied with one another to lavish praise upon him, and with complete sincerity. Of his rendition of Beethoven's Ninth Symphony one critic asserted, "He is the unique interpreter of his work." Puccini, referring to the way in which he had led the performance of *Fanciulla*, said, "Toscanini has composed this opera a second time." Another world authority spoke of Toscanini and Wagner in these memorable words: "Toscanini's conducting of Wagner here and abroad has always left in the minds of the susceptible the same unshaken conviction; that this was Wagner's music as he himself had dared to dream that it might sound."

To all this praise and adulation Toscanini seemed to turn a deaf ear. Essentially he is a very modest man and he gives the credit to the composers and to the musicians who work with him. He says he is "merely the bridge between the two." After a concert or a tour, he will wrap himself in a cloak of aloofness and retreat to his family and a small group of friends or to his piano and his scores.

The musicians of other countries were casting envious eyes now toward Milan and Turin, where he also conducted a great deal. They would go to almost any length to entice him from Italy and pry him away from Milan.

The Metropolitan Opera Company in New York City caught him at last in 1908 at an opportune moment and brought him there for the opening of the season in November.

Particularly persuasive had been the pleading of Gatti-Casazza, with whom Toscanini had worked in Milan.

The New York critics were beside themselves. They could scarcely find enough adjectives to describe the brilliance of the new conductor. He was "an artist, an interpreter, a re-creator in the best sense." He was an "incomparable interpreter." He was "the finest," "the greatest," "the best" they had ever heard or seen.

But Toscanini's passion for perfection earned him enemies, too. Rehearsals were long and often stormy. The demands upon singers and musicians were numerous and exacting. Batons were sometimes broken and angry words shot through the air. Many a star threatened to resign or not to sing. And many a musician rebelled against this perfectionist. But the results were incredible in brilliancy of tone, in depth of understanding, in quality of acting. Great music and outstanding opera was produced and somehow most of the rebels stayed on to work under this master musician.

Then came World War I. These momentous years of opera under the maestro's leadership were over. His son was in the service and Toscanini felt it his patriotic duty to return to Italy. Once back in his native land, he led concert after concert for the men, often within the battle lines. This was his contribution to the building of morale; his part in the war. Once in a while he even conducted community sings in various parts of the country. The proceeds of his concerts were given to war charities.

Even in wartime his nationalism was not narrow. Italy might be fighting Germany, but the Italian music lovers were not fighting the great German composers of times past or present.

Music is international. Toscanini was convinced on this point even if all Italians were not.

At a soldiers' benefit concert in Rome in 1916, Toscanini had hardly begun the Funeral March from Wagner's *Götterdämmerung* when the audience rebelled. At the top of their voices some of them shrieked, "Stop him! Stop him!" And from other parts of the angry audience came the barbed query, "Who is it for—the German or the Italian soldiers?" Livid, Toscanini turned and shouted, "I am playing music that belongs to the world." Incensed at the reaction of these superpatriots, he left the podium and did not return.

Once the war was finally over, he assembled an orchestra of the very best Italian musicians and started out on a trip to the United States and Canada. Theirs was a succession of successes. In six months they played 124 concerts and their stay was prolonged beyond its original length. In New York City music lovers demanded a minimum of ten concerts instead of the three that were scheduled. At the close of the tour Pierre Monteux expressed the feelings of most American conductors when he asserted, "we are all mere striplings compared to him."

During the war La Scala had been closed. Plans were afoot to reopen it as soon after the war as possible, and to overhaul and renovate the famous building. Toscanini was the only one whom they really wanted as conductor. His conditions were exacting, but they were met. In 1921 he returned to Milan for the opening night,—on December 26 with the opera *Falstaff* by his beloved friend Verdi.

For eight years he brought incomparable music to La Scala. He played *Die Meistersinger, Mefistofele, Boris Godunov, The Magic Flute, Fidelio, Tristan and Isolde* and *Aïda* over and over. He revived *Pelléas and Mélisande* in memory of Debussy. He directed the old favorites, *Das Rheingold* and *Die Walküre*, many, many times. He revived *Don Carlos* and *Der Freischütz* and conducted Gounod's *Faust* and Verdi's *Falstaff* in many incredible performances.

Behind closed doors the players and singers rehearsed. Often Toscanini was violent, dictatorial. He was a little volcano, ever ready to erupt. But he knew what he wanted, and even though batons snapped and musical scores sometimes soared in the air, the results were magnificent. There was a proximity to perfection that stunned those who knew nothing of the long, tedious hours of rehearsals, the exacting demands of the conductor, the incredible memory of the maestro, and his uncanny ability to spot a single player the slightest bit off key. And behind the rehearsals were hours and days in which the maestro pored over the biographies of the composers so that he might saturate himself in the spirit in which their music was composed.

The music he brought forth from his musicians was often moving. But some occasions stood out in the minds of those who heard him often. One was the homage he paid to his old friend Puccini on December 3, 1924, when he conducted the funeral elegy from Puccini's *Edgar* during the memorial service for this great composer in the Milan Cathedral. This was his final tribute to a great and loyal friend. It was magnificent music, moving music.

Not only was Toscanini heard in the various cities in Italy. He was also heard in the capitals of all European countries. One of the finest tours which he ever took was in 1929, just before he left La Scala. The houses were sold out many days

in advance in Vienna and Berlin, for this was to be his valedictory to Europe. The concerts there were exciting and the
crowds enthusiastic. Toscanini was not just an Italian conductor; he was now the maestro of world music. He belonged
to music lovers everywhere.

Up until 1929 Toscanini had been a conductor of operas.
Now he was to become primarily a conductor of symphonies.
For years the United States had been trying to get him to come
back to their shores, and at last he yielded to their entreaties.
The orchestra that he was to lead was the New York Philharmonic. With them he was to remain from 1926 until 1936,
spending his winters in New York City as their conductor, and
his summers at the famed festivals at Bayreuth, Germany, and
Salzburg, Austria. Under his direction the New York Philharmonic was to become the leading orchestra in the world.

Soon Europe was clamoring to see and hear Toscanini, and
in 1930 he agreed to a tour with the New York orchestra. It
was a triumph. There were twenty-three concerts—in Zurich,
Milan, Turin, Rome, Florence, Munich, Vienna, Budapest,
Prague, Leipzig, Dresden, Berlin, Brussels, and London. Everywhere people were thrilled by the best music of the world
under the best conductor anywhere and with the best orchestra
that there was.

Meanwhile Toscanini had been invited to Bayreuth in 1930
to conduct at that famed Wagnerian shrine. This invitation
shook the musical world. This was the center of Wagnerian
music and as such it was *echt Deutsch*—pure German. To
invite a non-German to conduct and later to become artistic
director was a sacrilege in the eyes of some. Had there been

any doubt as to the wisdom of the invitation, however, it vanished before the scintillating performances of this devotee of Wagner. His renditions of *Tannhäuser* and *Parsifal* in the first season, and of all the other magnificent works of Wagner in the years that followed, removed any doubts as to the wisdom of the choice except for a few die-hards.

Then came 1933 and Hitler's rise to power. Toscanini had listened as a boy to his father's stories of being a soldier in Garibaldi's army. Ever since that time he had been an ardent opponent of tyranny, despotism, and fascism. In 1933 he had signed a petition appealing to Hitler to stop the persecution of musicians and others on racial, religious, and political grounds.

So in 1933 he said "No" to the invitation to go to Bayreuth. He would not conduct music in Hitler's Germany—even at his beloved Bayreuth. Hitler sent a special invitation to the world's outstanding conductor. But this infuriated him still further. He declined "because of painful events which have wounded my feelings as a man and as an artist." To others Toscanini tartly remarked, "I burn or I freeze, but I cannot be lukewarm." Everyone knew his temperature at this point.

He turned, then, in 1934 and 1935 to Salzburg, Austria—the birthplace of Mozart—as the new Bayreuth, the new summer center of world music. Significantly, he chose Mendelssohn's *Reformation Symphony* for one of the concerts. What better choice than the work of a great Jewish composer to show the world how he felt about racial and religious persecution?

This work depicts the struggle for religious liberty in sixteenth century Europe, and the composer's works were of course banned in Hitler Germany.

There were opera works, too, at Salzburg, such as Verdi's *Falstaff* and Beethoven's *Fidelio*. And to interpret these great works were the Vienna Philharmonic Orchestra and outstanding singers like Lotte Lehmann. To further stress the worldwide nature of music, Toscanini broadcast one concert of music by Wagner and Mendelssohn to the United States.

For the concerts in 1933, 1935, 1936, and 1937 crowds from all over the world converged at Salzburg. The audiences were international and so was the music. These persons were gathered from all over the globe to speak the common language of great music.

Trouble for Toscanini brewed at home, too. A dictator ruled Italy and from musicians he demanded tribute as well as from all others. Such tribute Toscanini would not pay and he paid the price for his convictions.

In 1931 he had been asked to conduct a concert of the works of Martucci in Bologna. He accepted. At that time it was understood the *Giovanezza*, a Fascist piece, would always be played at the beginning of a concert. But Toscanini did not conform. To have done so would have meant that he had buckled under to Fascism. So at the close of the concert he was waylaid and seriously injured.

A few days later a resolution was passed by the artists and musicians of that city, censuring Toscanini for his lack of patriotism. After that incident he refused to conduct in his native land and fled from Italy. He vowed that he would not return as long as the Fascists ruled—and he did not, until after World War II.

In 1936 Toscanini resigned from the Philharmonic, intending to retire. A farewell concert was arranged and a queue waited for ten hours in order to purchase tickets for this final concert. But it was not time for him to retire. He had too much to give and the world needed him far too much.

Over in Palestine the Jewish community had organized a symphony orchestra, composed of many refugees from central Europe. Toscanini was anxious to help them and, by so doing, to focus attention on their plight and on the injustice which had caused it. So he and his wife flew to Palestine and on December 26—that special date in his public life—opened the season with a concert at Tel Aviv.

Europe had known and acclaimed him as a native son. North America had adopted him as an Italian-American. South America had given him his first boost and had welcomed him back on several tours. Now the Near East had a chance to catch a glimpse of him, even if it were only a fleeting one. It made the most of the opportunity, almost worshiping him on this trip to Palestine.

New Yorkers had been loath to see Toscanini leave, and they were anxious to lure him back. Music lovers had multiplied in the last few years and millions wanted to hear the Toscanini concerts. There was only one medium by which he could reach those millions. That was radio.

The National Broadcasting Company was alert to the situation. It arranged to assemble the world's greatest symphony orchestra if Toscanini would conduct. The possibilities in such a scheme intrigued the maestro, and he yielded to their entreaties to return.

On Christmas night of 1937 millions of persons clustered around their radios and, in the glow of the multicolored lights of Christmas trees, listened to the NBC orchestra. Since that memorable night increasingly large audiences have listened to the music of Brahms and Beethoven, Chopin and Cherubini, Grieg and Grofé, Hadyn and Handel, Strauss and Smetana, Weber and Wagner, and a host of newer composers as interpreted or introduced by the talented Toscanini.

One other medium of mass communication beckoned to him—the motion pictures. But here Toscanini balked. Fabulous sums were offered if he would film even short educational movies. But he would not budge. His mind was made up. He was adamant.

Only once did he break that resolve. That time it was for a very special reason. World War II was raging and the maestro was eager to do what he could for the Allied cause. His passion for freedom had not abated. With trepidation the officials of the Office of War Information approached him to appear in a film for use overseas. Toscanini agreed to such a film. For the central composition he appropriately chose Verdi's *Inno delle Nazione* or Hymn to the Nations.

For this thirty-minute film he assembled the NBC orchestra; Jan Peerce, tenor from the Metropolitan Opera Company; and the Westminster Choir of ninety voices, a special music school from Princeton University. For weeks Studio 8H at Radio City reverberated with the rich, sonorous notes of violins, the strident bars from cornets and French horns, the lyrical notes of harps, and the melodious, full tones of bassoons and oboes. The men were absorbed in the preparations for filming the story of Italy's fight against her oppressors in the nineteenth century, which Toscanini considered parallel with the present.

Finally the great day arrived and the cameras were rolled in, the lenses focused, the lights arranged, and the film shot. The music was recorded and the joint project soon sent on its way by auto and truck and airplane and jeep to the far corners of the earth.

Meanwhile classical music had proved its popularity as a daily menu for soldiers and civilians in a world at war. Every night at 20:30 Greenwich Time, the Toscanini Hour could be heard from Naples,—a full sixty minutes of recordings by Toscanini and the various orchestras he had conducted since his first recording in 1920.

VE and VJ days passed and the Toscanini Hour was discontinued. But every Sunday night in the winter crowds flocked into Studio 8H at Radio City to see the sharp-eyed, stern-looking Italian genius mount the podium shortly after 5 P.M. and quickly begin an hour of musical excellence. With dispatch he catches the eyes of his musicians, raises his baton, and the concert is on. The eyes of the audience shift from instrument to instrument, from player to player. Eventually they settle on the maestro, with his white hair concentrated along the sides of his head and curling slightly at the back, his little mustache, his trim black clothes, and his graceful hands.

Then the eyes of the audience shift to his baton and his left hand. He conducts almost as much with that hand as with the right one. His large left palm is raised and the thumb extended at a right angle. Then he brings the hand slowly to his face and the forefinger almost touches his mustache. Meanwhile the right hand is signaling entrances, keeping time, indicating shadings of meaning.

Often it is the large circular motions with the baton pointing towards the floor which catch the eye of the concertgoer.

The maestro looks for a moment as if he is stirring his caldron and the concoctions he conjures up are enchanting. Then his eyes are almost closed and his forehead is ruffled as he strives for lighter, softer tone, more nebulous effects—a murmur or whisper from the orchestra.

And most of the time his mouth is moving as he hums the music of the orchestra. Unconsciously his body is bent forward, firm yet relaxed, as if pleading and saying, "Everything must sing—everything."

In farmhouse parlors, penthouse apartments, plantation houses and California ranches, in speeding autos, streamline trains, and luxuriant planes millions of devotees and novices are listening to the world's greatest music from the world's greatest conductor.

Such was the scene on Sunday nights all through the 1930s and 1940s and even into the fifties. A nation had caught the Toscanini madness. He became a hero to millions of people who were hearing fine music for the first time through the medium of the radio. If only they could see him in person, they thought.

Fortunately their desire coincided with a desire which he had to see more of his adopted country and to share good music with its people.

On April 17, 1950, the Toscanini train left New York City for a transcontinental tour. Before they returned, the maestro and his musicians were to cover more than eight thousand miles and to give concerts in twenty cities. First they went south, and then west, performing in Baltimore, Richmond, Atlanta, New Orleans, Dallas, Los Angeles, San Francisco, Seattle, Denver, and other major cities. The tour concluded with a concert in the nation's capital with an audience that included President Truman and his family and many of the leading officials in the national government.

Wherever the orchestra played the concert halls, theaters, or auditoriums were sold out long in advance. People were thrilled to see this "legend" come to life. Toscanini became "the barnstormer with a baton," as one correspondent called him.

And Toscanini was thrilled, too. In Williamsburg he inspected the colonial town which has been restored by the Rockefellers. In New Orleans he visited the jazz spots. In Sun Valley he took a trip up Baldy Mountain in a ski tow.

He was eighty-three when he took this trip—but he acted like a boy. He enjoyed every minute of the journey. And when he returned, he gave a lawn party at his home in Riverdale, a suburb of New York City, to thank his fellow voyagers for their part in the happiest and most memorable tour he had ever taken.

Meanwhile another medium had opened up which would take Toscanini into the homes of millions of Americans—and perhaps eventually into the homes of people in other parts of the world. This was television. In 1947 he conducted his first concert over TV and in succeeding years the first concert in each series has been telecast to the nation.

All through these years he has led a strenuous life. Some people have wondered how he could do it. Martin Gumpert, a doctor and an authority on geriatrics, or old age, has this to say about Toscanini's energy, "His secret is unlimited devotion to a limited area of life. Creative passion enlarges the frame of existence almost beyond the point of death. Indeed, it sometimes seems that death will wait until a powerful drive toward some goal has been achieved."

Another explanation seems to lie in his ability to relax and enjoy life when he is not on the job. Most of his spare time is spent at Villa Pauline, a twenty-one room house on an eight acre estate in the outskirts of New York City. There he lives quite simply and enjoys playing the piano and listening to records. He has become quite a television fan and especially enjoys prize fights. Some of his time is spent in romping with his grandchildren or playing jokes on members of the family and guests in his home, of whom there are many. Often he indulges in late hours and passes the time discussing politics and art with his friends.

He is an incredible person. As Carl Engel, chief of the Music Division of the Library of Congress, once said, "So striking a phenomenon as Toscanini is hardly explicable by known laws. He is one of those splendid anomalies whereby nature, from time to time, designs to rehabilitate the human race."

Such is the story of Toscanini, the master musician, the maestro of world music, one of the truly great leaders of the world today.

MATHILDA WREDE

Friend of Prisoners

Should she contradict the speaker or remain silent? He was the director of criminal work in France and internationally famous. She was just an ordinary prison worker in Finland and not known outside her own country.

Did she dare to challenge this prominent person? He was a man at a convention made up almost entirely of men. She was a woman and women were supposed to be sentimental and unrealistic about prison work.

Should she say what was true? He was a veteran and she was only twenty-six years old. His lecture had been brilliantly written and eloquently delivered. She would express herself poorly, especially in French.

These were the questions which disturbed Mathilda Wrede as she sat as a delegate to the International Penal Congress in Petrograd, Russia, in 1890.

The paper which had just been read was, "The Treatment of Incorrigible Criminals." In it the speaker had said that there were many prisoners for whom nothing could be done. They were incurable—incorrigible. Society was wasting its time, energy, and money on such men and women.

Mathilda Wrede had come to the Congress to listen and to learn from the leaders in this field. But such statements were untrue, even if they were made by so-called authorities.

Her thoughts flashed back to the men and women she knew in Finland. People had called them incurable and incorrigible, too. But today many of them were no longer prisoners. They were free persons leading normal lives in various parts of her homeland.

Gradually the applause died down and the speaker stepped back to his seat on the platform. Her mind was made up. She could not keep quiet. Such a message could not be taken back to the four corners of the earth without being challenged. She asked for permission to speak and was granted that privilege.

Nervously she advanced to the front of the room, uncertain as to the exact words but certain as to the general idea that she wanted to get across to this large audience from all over the world. The hall became quiet, deathly quiet, she thought. She summoned her courage, and began to speak.

"Friends," she said, "we have listened to a brilliant paper by one of our leading authorities on work with prisoners. Each of us has learned something from his remarkable presentation. But I beg to disagree with him on one essential point.

"My experience is not as great as his, but I have worked with thousands of prisoners of every kind in the prisons of Finland. My experience has convinced me that there is no such thing as an incurable criminal. It has led me to the firm belief that there is no person who is absolutely incorrigible."

These were challenging statements and her colleagues listened in rapt attention to this courageous woman.

"There is one means," she continued, "by which every criminal can be transformed. That means is the power of God. Laws and systems cannot change the heart of a single criminal, but God can. I am persuaded that above all else and far more than before, we must concern ourselves with the souls of prisoners and with their spiritual lives."

She paused a moment as if to catch her breath and then started to leave the platform. The room echoed with applause. At first she felt that the applause came from courtesy rather than from agreement with her ideas. But when it continued, she thought that there were probably others who had wanted to say what she had said, but had kept quiet.

Later she was to learn how many had agreed with her.

In a very short time she received an invitation to a formal dinner in the Winter Palace with other delegates at the Congress. She declined. It seemed incongruous to her for a person working with the poorest members of society to dress in lavish evening clothes and dine and wine in such surroundings. Even when she was told that her place was to be at the Czar's table, she graciously said that she would be unable to go.

An acceptance would harm her work among the prisoners and their families and she would do nothing that would hinder that work. Faced with a choice of displeasing the Czar or her prisoner friends, she would displease the Czar.

As the Congress continued, it was increasingly evident that she was being watched by the secret police. She was a Finn and Finland was under the domination of Russia. She was interested in prisoners, including those who had been put in jail for political reasons. Furthermore, she was outspoken, fearless. Was it any wonder that she was being watched?

Her friends were afraid that she would be imprisoned herself and that her work in Finland would be interrupted. At all costs that must not happen. Finally, at their earnest entreaty, she left the Congress before it was adjourned and returned to Finland.

These incidents are typical of the life of Finland's greatest prison reformer. Like Elizabeth Fry of England, an earlier crusader in this field, Mathilda Wrede had worked closely with all kinds of prisoners. She was concerned with conditions in the prisons. She was interested in better food, more adequate clothing, better trained prison guards. She wanted to establish classes in the prisons and encourage the men to read and study while they were there so that they would be better prepared for life outside when they were released.

But more important than any of these things was their mental and spiritual health. Unless someone could change their attitudes towards themselves, towards their families and friends, and towards society, all these other things would be worthless.

Her job, as she saw it, was to counsel with the prisoners and their families. She must help them to gain a more positive attitude towards themselves and others. She must give them faith in themselves and a feeling that someone cared about them, no matter what they had done.

In order to do a better job, she lived in humble quarters and ate the simple meals that the poorer classes ate. In this way she could understand better how they felt. And in this way she could save money to help the prisoners and their families.

Such a life was absolutely new to her. Her background had been as a member of a wealthy family of the Finnish nobility. But she had renounced all this because of her interest in prison work.

In order to understand Mathilda Wrede better, let us review

her life and the events which caused her to change her mode of living so radically.

She was born in Vaasa, on the western coast of Finland, on March 8, 1864, the ninth child in the family of Baron Carl Gustav Wrede and Baroness Eleonora Glansenstjerna Wrede. Her father was governor of the Vaasa district, a position he held for many years. Her mother died when Mathilda was eleven years old and her oldest sister, Helena, became "mother" to her. For Helena she always retained a deep affection. In later years they became boon companions.

As a child Mathilda was frail and delicate. Consequently her family encouraged her to lead an outdoor life as much as was possible in that climate. Her formal education was for the most part with tutors, although she attended a boarding school in Fredrikshamn (Hamina) and spent a year in one of the Finnish folk schools. She had a quick mind and her lessons were not hard for her. Her greatest difficulty seemed to be in making friends.

She was extremely fond of animals and liked horses in particular. This led to an interest in later life in the Society for the Prevention of Cruelty to Animals.

It was the custom in those days for prisoners to be used on the estates of political officials. Since her father was a governor, a good many prisoners were brought to their home to work around the place.

One day when she was seven years old she was waiting for her tutor to arrive when she saw a prisoner across the street having the chain on his ankle soldered. When the tutor arrived, he quickly pulled Mathilda away from the window.

Children were not supposed to see such sights. Mathilda protested, saying, "If the prisoner can bear it, I can certainly bear to see it."

Two years later the family was planning a picnic. This was to be a "spring breakfast" which the townspeople always held when the birds began to come back to Finland from their winter in the south. Mathilda refused to go. At first she would not give any reason. Then, when they pressed her for an explanation, she told them that she did not want to see the prisoners whom they would pass on their way to the picnic grounds.

Her father protested that they would be hidden by the prison's high walls. But Mathilda was adamant. She knew that they were there,—walls or no walls. A compromise was finally reached and the family proceeded to the picnic by another path.

A few years later the lock on her bedroom door was broken and a prisoner was called to fix it. A short time before that event Mathilda had had a deep religious experience and she told the prisoner about it. She was astonished at his interest and his friendliness. Telling the story about him years later, she said, "I found much that was good in this man."

Perhaps that short, simple statement was her basic philosophy about people. She found much that was good in everyone she met. And because she looked for the good rather than the evil in people, she brought out the best that was in them. She had learned this early in life.

As a result of this talk with the prisoner, she promised to visit him in the prison on the next Sunday. Her father was shocked by such a plan. It was ridiculous, he said, for a young girl to visit prisoners. It was unbecoming for one of her sex and for the daughter of a nobleman. Besides, it was dangerous.

Mathilda, however, saw all this quite differently. She had made a promise and she intended to keep it. The man had been friendly and there was no reason why she should not be friendly in return. Perhaps that was what he needed most. She was a resolute person and did not intend to give in. Finally her father agreed to the visit if the warden would accompany her. That was the agreement they reached—and Mathilda visited her friend in prison.

This was only the first of a series of visits there. The other prisoners seemed glad to see someone, and gradually she began to visit with several of the men rather than just with the one man.

Then an important event took place in her life. A minister who had meant a great deal to her wrote that he was coming to visit Mathilda and her family. She had already promised the prisoners that she would pay a visit to them that day. She was torn between the two engagements. That evening she was reading the Bible and came across the words in Jeremiah, "Behold I cannot speak for I am a child. But the Lord said unto me, 'Say not, I am a child, for thou shalt go to all that I shall send thee, and whatsoever I command thee, thou shalt speak.'"

Some people would say that it was merely a coincidence that she turned to that statement. But Mathilda Wrede felt otherwise. She felt that she had received an answer to her problem. Her promise to the prisoners should come first. So the next day she made her regular visit to her friends there.

No sooner had she gotten started in this work than her

father resigned as governor and the family moved to their estate at Rabbelun, quite a distance away. That seemed to end her prison work.

Then, one day on a trip to the capital, Helsinki (it was called Helsingfors then), she saw a squad of prisoners working on the street. This prompted her to go to the Chief Inspector of Finnish prisons. From him she requested a permit to visit the various penal and convict prisons of Finland. As she put it, if there were no prisons where she lived, she would travel to the prisons.

During her visit in Helsinki she visited the prison there. A short time later she went to Villanstrand and Kakola in other parts of Finland. This latter institution was the largest in the country and the one in which the worst offenders were kept.

Thus, at the age of twenty, Mathilda Wrede began to pioneer in prison work. Such work was badly needed in Finland in those days, but it was also difficult and daring work, for women had not carried on such activities in that country before her time.

Also, the prisons of Finland were far more barbarous and lonely than they are today. Prisoners often wore body irons or an iron harness with a belt and collar attached by chains in front and in back, and iron wrist chains which were attached to the entire apparatus by smaller chains. The insane and those bordering on insanity were put into the same cells as relatively normal persons. Habitual criminals and first-termers were treated exactly alike and were thrown together regularly.

Mathilda Wrede went into such wretched dungeons to bring hope to those who were without hope, courage to those who were afraid, friendship to those who were lonely, and good will to those who were unloved. Oftentimes the experiences she had were harrowing ones. The worst incident was the attempt of a heavily chained half-insane prisoner to strangle her. She looked this man straight in the eye and quietly said to him, "Your intention will not be carried out." Her presence of mind and her calm saved her.

Another time she decided to visit an inmate whom the chaplain said was "made of leather—nothing makes any impression." As usual she went alone. The prisoner was surprised to see her visiting him without the warden and astonished when she insisted that he sit down beside her in the cell.

Suddenly he turned to her and said, "And do you know how that big dent got into my wall there?"

"No," she replied, "I don't have any idea how that happened."

Boastfully he said, "When I was still allowed to work in my cell, I used to work at carpentry. One day when the warden came in, I had made up my mind to kill him. So I took my ax and aimed it at his head. But the blade flew off and into that wall."

Then he changed the subject abruptly, asking, "Aren't you afraid of me? Don't you know who I am?"

"No," she answered him quietly, "I am not the least afraid, although I know who you are, for I am sure that you do not mean to harm me. Besides, God is with me and while he watches over me, I have nothing to fear."

The prisoner was overwhelmed by her generosity and trust. Turning to her, he said, "I thought there wasn't a single creature who cared about me. And now you have come and showed me kindness. You tell me God loves me. I suppose you are a

Christian. Well, I should like to be one, too, if that is possible."

After these remarks, he rose quickly, rattled his chains, and shouted, "If it is true that God forgives us, why don't men forgive us, too? In these chains I'll grow worse till I am altogether a devil."

Calmly and confidently Mathilda Wrede talked to him and finally he grew calm, too. Eventually she won from him a promise to contribute what he could to the prison in which he was doomed to spend his life.

It was her firm conviction that even under prison conditions men could contribute to the world. She believed in a kind of chain reaction of good thoughts. This is how she expressed it: "Do you know that every one of us, if he wants to, can improve the world somewhat? We improve the world with good, clear thoughts and we retard the progress of the world with our hateful, dark thoughts. As you lie here thinking, 'The warden is an evil person,' or 'The director is unjust,' you weave a net of hate and bitterness. When you think of your wife and children at home, then your thoughts are higher and you weave a net of friendliness and love. If we all thought good thoughts, the air would be perceptibly warmer and it would pass further and further. Such thoughts move like waves and perhaps eventually reach our loved ones as signs of our love.

"There are likewise still higher thoughts, the highest possible thoughts, which can reach into eternity and unto God. I speak from experience. I am a Wrede and my thoughts are passionate and strong. I have fought against harsh and bitter thoughts and I know that they have done others harm as well as harming my own soul and the spirit of God. But I also can think other thoughts—those of love—and broadcast them. Often I have received from others similar thoughts. In a similar way you, too, can come into communion with your heavenly Father. When we remain in contact with Him, listen to Him and attempt to set forth His love, then we belong to those who help the world forward to light, peace, and goodness."

Her philosophy was simple. It was so simple that some people are tempted to say that she was naïve. But it worked. She was able to do things that other more sophisticated people could not or would not do. She was able to face situations that most people could not face. She was able to communicate confidence and build respect in those prison friends of hers. What more could anyone ask of a person's philosophy of life?

She was constantly seeking ways of helping individual prisoners. One young man confided to her that he could not recall one good deed he had ever done. Certainly she could help him, she thought. Over in the corner of the cell she spied a mug of stale beer. "I am so thirsty," she said. "I wonder if you would be so kind as to give me something to drink?" He hesitated, then gave her the cup, fully expecting that she would decline it.

When she took it, drank from it, and thanked him, he was taken back. "Oh no," he said, "I am the one who ought to thank you."

Her work was of a serious nature, but she often approached it with a sense of humor. When she was invited to court, one of her friends asked her, "And what dress will you wear, Mathilda?" With a quick smile she answered, "Oh I think I'll wear the newer one." She only owned two dresses.

One of her prisoners insisted that he just couldn't keep from stealing. So Mathilda Wrede's advice to him was to steal thereafter only in her house, so he could bring back the stolen objects the next day.

Perhaps it was partly this quiet humor that endeared her to the prisoners and their families. Certainly it helped her to live through many times of stress and strain.

On her birthday in 1886 her father took her for a walk along the river front. When they reached one of the nearby farms, her father told her that that piece of ground and the house were to be her birthday present. This was to be a home for discharged prisoners, a kind of rehabilitation center.

As the years rolled by, she was to spend more and more time there. After all, the really important job was to help discharged prisoners to adjust to life outside the prison. Otherwise they would be back in jail within a few months.

But it was not always easy to work with these men who had been in prison so long. One spring she asked Lanquist, one of the former prisoners, to roll the fields on this little farm. "Who will help me?" was his immediate reply.

"One man ought to be able to do that job alone," was her reply.

"Oh yes," he sneered, "that's the way the gentry talk."

"Very well," she said, "I will roll the field myself."

At 5 A.M. she started to work and at 7:00 in the evening the work was done. Some of the men offered to help her when they saw that she meant what she had said. But she was determined to do the job alone. And she did it, too.

From that time on there was little trouble over such requests or suggestions. She had shown that she was not above doing what had to be done. She had shamed the men by her own action.

She was not always so successful, however. Pekonen, one of her prison friends, wanted to go to the United States to start life over again. But he lacked money for the trip. Mathilda Wrede finally brought herself to the point where she could sell her favorite horse, Reima, to raise the necessary funds. The day of Pekonen's departure came and he arrived at the Wrede home to say farewell and urge her not to come to the pier on such a rainy, miserable day. Contrary to her usual custom in such cases, she did not accompany him to the boat, but gave him the money at her house.

Later in the day she was walking down town and saw a drunken man whose appearance was familiar. She followed him into a tavern. As a woman she was out of place there and was asked immediately what she wanted.

"I am looking for a man named Pekonen," she answered. "Could you help me?"

They pointed to the corner of the tavern. There he was. There was Pekonen, for whom she had sold her most prized personal possession. Eventually he did get to the United States, but he did not stay long. He returned to Finland to spend the rest of his life.

Koponen was a somewhat similar case. He had been exiled to Siberia. He escaped from imprisonment there and made his way mile by mile across the endless, desolate plain, through the thick black forests, across the swampy marshes to Finland.

Finally he reached his native land and hid near the farmhouse of a wealthy farmer. When night came, he stole up to the house and found the door unlocked. The family was asleep.

How quiet and peaceful this was! How different from Siberia. He could not steal in this place.

But within a short time the desire to steal got the better of him: he entered a monastery and stole. Then he became troubled. After all, he had intended to start life over again and to give up stealing. Remembering his old friend, he went to see Mathilda Wrede.

She advised him to return to Siberia. "You cannot start over again by doing wrong. You escaped from prison and that was wrong. You have stolen again and that was wrong. If you return to Siberia, I shall petition the Senate for a pardon. Then you will be legally free."

It was a difficult decision to make, but he decided to return to Siberia. Otherwise he would always be an escaped convict hiding from the law. So he started on the long journey back to Siberia. Partway back he gave himself up to the police and was taken off to prison.

But Mathilda Wrede did not forget her promise. She intervened on his behalf and finally secured his release. But Koponen vanished. She never saw or heard from him again. Her only satisfaction was in the fact that he had secured his release by legal rather than illegal methods. Somewhere he was a free man again.

Much of her time was spent in the prisons, but her work was not limited to such activities. The summer months were largely spent visiting the families of the prisoners or seeing the ones who had returned to their homes. She would travel all over Finland to see these friends of hers.

This was good for her as well as for them. The work in the winter was strenuous and confining. Mathilda Wrede was not a vigorous, healthy person and she would be worn out by the time that summer rolled around. Traveling across the lakes or passing through the woods and living in the out of doors gave her new vitality. It also gave her fresh hope and inspiration. She reveled in the beauty of the Finnish countryside. Then in the winter she could reflect on her visits and the beauty of the landscapes she had seen. Such pictures in her mind were important if she was to remain calm and confident as she listened to the gruesome stories of prisoners and saw the conditions under which they lived.

These visits also gave her a feeling of accomplishment. It was good to see prisoners who were adjusting to their new life. It was gratifying to have them invite their neighbors and friends in to meet her. Even a great spirit like Mathilda Wrede had to have the sense of achievement to keep going. She, too, needed to know that progress was being made, even if it was slow and slight.

In 1912 all this work in the prisons came to an abrupt end. She had tried to improve the conditions in the hospital of one of the prisons, but without any success. She had gone to the prison doctor but had not won her point. She had seen the prison chaplain, but he was not willing to help. She had talked to the governor, but without making any progress. She had pleaded with the Prison Board, but they had not been budged.

In despair she told her story to a journalist and he had written a story of conditions in Finnish prisons. The public had been aroused and made protests to those in charge of the prisons.

But the prison authorities were incensed. They curtailed her work and told her she could not visit any prisoner without some official going with her. In her mind that was impossible. Most of the value of her work would be destroyed if an official had to accompany her. The prisoners would no longer feel free to talk with her. She could no longer establish the intimate, confidential relationship with them which she had had before.

She could not accept this arrangement. She declined to visit under such restrictions.

But there were others who needed her help. As she put it, "Cut off from prisoners, my heart opened for others—for all men and women who are prisoners and as much in need of love and help as those behind prison bars."

World War I had begun. That meant that there was work for her to do. There were families of Finnish soldiers to be helped. There were people hard hit by rising prices who needed assistance. She turned her attention to these and other needy families.

Then in 1917 war broke out in Finland. Many people called it the War of Liberation because it was an attempt on the part of the Finns to overthrow Russian rule and win their independence. But Mathilda Wrede called it the Civil War. She insisted that no war that destroyed so many people and so much property and loosed so much hatred and bitterness could be called a War of Liberation.

She refused to take sides in the conflict. Instead, she would help the victims of both sides. Her family was of the nobility and therefore sided with the "whites." But most of the people with whom she had spent her life were "reds." Perhaps she could perform a special service by aiding people on both sides. She could serve as a conciliator between the warring factions in her homeland.

Symbolically she kept a small vase on the table in her sitting room. In the vase were two roses—one red, the other white. "Each is beautiful," she said. "Each needs the same sunshine and the same water, but the beauty of the one enhances the beauty of the other, and they agree very well in my vase."

There were not many people who could play such a role. She could. People understood her position and her reasons for not taking sides. Occasionally people from the "red" and "white" sides of the conflict would find themselves in her house at the same time.

One day, for example, the mother and wife of an imprisoned "white" minister were visiting her when three "red" leaders appeared. She sent the men to a bedroom to wait until she had finished her first conference. Then some Salvation Army workers came to talk to her about the identification of the unknown dead. She left both groups to talk for a moment to this third party. Fortunately each remained in its assigned place so that they would not have to meet. Meanwhile Mathilda Wrede was helping them all.

When permission was again granted to her to resume her prison work, she no longer had the physical strength to become acquainted with the large numbers of new prisoners who had entered these institutions in the time since she had previously visited them. She decided that she could not take up this same type of work again.

But she did continue to work with former prisoners throughout the length and breadth of Finland.

After the war she became more active in work for temperance, in the protection of minority groups, and in the promotion of international peace.

In 1919 she was one of a small group of peace leaders from various countries who held an international conference in Bilthoven in the Netherlands. There they formed the Fellowship of Reconciliation, an international association devoted to the furtherance of peace. In that group she was to be very active for the few remaining years of her life. Tension between Finland and Russia was to continue, and because of her unique background, she was able to serve often as an interpreter and reconciler between these two opposing groups.

Then, too, she became more and more interested in the rights of minority groups. One such group was the Greek Orthodox priests who had a monastery on an island of Lake Ladoga. They were being forced to celebrate Easter at the same time and in the same way as the western Christian churches of Finland. They objected, but to no avail.

Mathilda Wrede felt that this was an absolute infringement of the freedom of conscience guaranteed by the Finnish Constitution. So she championed their cause, even though she was not a member of the Greek Orthodox Church. She appealed to the Finnish government, to the World Alliance for Promoting Friendship through the Churches, and eventually to the League of Nations. Her efforts in this case were successful after a long and strenuous campaign.

Also, many persons were fleeing from the religious and political purges in Russia. Finland was close by and hundreds of them managed to get across the border to that land. Most of them arrived, however, without food, without adequate clothing, and without any prospects of work.

These people needed help and Mathilda Wrede organized her friends in Finland to help these refugees. They supplied food and clothing and shelter for them and tried to find jobs so that they could get a new start in life in Finland.

After a long illness, Mathilda Wrede died on Christmas Day, 1928. Her death came in one of the rooms in the House of Honor—a house which the women of Finland had given her on her sixtieth birthday.

Surrounding her in this house were some of the reminders of her work with prisoners. There was the white birch furniture which had been made by men in the prisons. On the mantelpiece was a bronze study of her favorite horse Reima, which she had sold to help Pekonen. There was a beautifully carved cabinet which a prisoner had made as a way of showing his gratitude to her. Many other intimate objects crowded the rooms where she had spent her last days and where she now lay in state.

On December 29 her body was removed from this house while the Salvation Army choir sang. It was taken to the Church of St. John where a motley crowd waited to pay tribute to her. Ordinary citizens were there, government officials, former convicts, refugees, Greek Orthodox priests, and the people of her neighborhood—in addition to members of her own family.

Of all the remarks made at the funeral, those of a former convict were probably the most touching. "Mathilda Wrede," he testified, "has been the mother confessor in prison to both criminal and political prisoners. To all she was equally indispensable. To all she was equally loving. We understood her because she belonged to us."

Turning to the coffin, he said, "Dry sand lies on your coffin together with beautiful flowers. These symbolize your life of service. You chose the sand of the human desert of need and during your lifetime you planted roses in this desert."

Many were reminded of the remarks made on her fiftieth birthday by another fellow countryman, who had said, "With her divining rod—love's divining rod—she has wandered over heath and desert. She has looked for the man in the murderer, the thief, and the cheat, in those scorned and abandoned by man and society, convinced that there is something of worth in every one. And certain it is that she again and again found hidden springs where no one else dreamed of their existence. Such work must at times meet with disappointment, but no good seed falls fruitless to the ground."

An Englishman, Henry Hodgkin, in the foreword of the only biography of Mathilda Wrede in English, said of her, "She has touched and healed and lifted those often thought of as untouchable, incurable, hopeless. Into no one knows how many broken lives she has brought the first ray of hope, because she dared to trust the 'untrustworthy.' She has had more confidence in many a one than he had in himself. She has poured out lavishly the riches of her faith and love in places where many would have counted them wasted."

She had spent almost all her time in one small country, but in that area she had practiced the principles of international good will. She had worked with the smallest units in the world community—individual men and women. But with them she had demonstrated the ideals which are needed in every community and in every nation. She had been a "friend of prisoners"—a citizen of the world.

DATE DUE

GAYLORD			PRINTED IN U.S.A.